Trueman, Stuart, 1911-
    Tall tales and true tales from down
east; eerie experiences, heroic exploits,
extraordinary personalities, ancient
legends and folklore from New Brunswick
and elsewhere in the Maritimes. Toronto,
McClelland and Stewart, 1979.
    171 p.

1. New Brunswick - Miscellanea. 2. Maritime
Provinces - Miscellanea. I. Title.
0771085982   087759X

STUART TRUEMAN

TALL TALES
AND
TRUE TALES
FROM
DOWN EAST

Eerie Experiences, Heroic Exploits, Extraordinary Personalities, Ancient Legends and Folklore from New Brunswick and Elsewhere in the Maritimes

McClelland and Stewart

ISBN: 0-7710-8598-2

The Canadian Publishers
McClelland and Stewart Limited
25 Hollinger Road, Toronto M4B 3G2

CANADIAN CATALOGUING IN PUBLICATION DATA

Trueman, Stuart, 1911-
    Tall tales and true tales from down east

ISBN 0-7710-8598-2

1. New Brunswick-Miscellanea.   2. Maritime
Provinces-Miscellanea.*   I. Title.

FC2461.8.T78   971.5'002   C79-094665-3
F1042.6.T78

"The Uninvited Bedfellow" previously appeared
in *The Atlantic Advocate*.

Printed and Bound in Canada

Contents

Books by Stuart Trueman

Cousin Elva, 1955; reissued in 1977 in paperback

The Ordeal of John Gyles, 1966; reissued in 1973 in paperback

You're Only as Old as You Act, 1969; Stephen Leacock Award for Humour

An Intimate History of New Brunswick, 1970; reissued in 1972 in paperback

My Life as a Rose-Breasted Grosbeak, 1972

The Fascinating World of New Brunswick, 1973

Ghost, Pirates and Treasure Trove, 1975

The Wild Life I've Led, 1976

TALL TALES
AND
TRUE TALES
FROM
DOWN EAST

Preface

The age-old Maritime Provinces, a fascinated American visitor once remarked, have 1,001 stories – and that's quite an understatement, as every Maritimer knows.

There are enough to fill a bookcase.

Some of the tales in this volume, mostly about New Brunswick, are told because they are in danger of slipping out of memory as the generations flash by, seemingly faster and faster.

For instance, the odd experiences that old-time Canadian customs men talked about at St. Stephen, across the St. Croix River from Calais, Maine.

No one realizes better than a customs officer what rascality may hide behind a jovial smile on an open honest face. Like the apple-cheeked young man who always drove a horse-and-carriage over the bridge and was greeted by the Canadian customs' routine question, "Have you anything to declare?"

"Only what you see," the youth laughingly replied, with a wave of his hand toward the empty carriage.

"Drive on," said the officer.

Not until long afterward did they learn the boy was smuggling U.S.-made carriages and horses into Canada – and, incredibly, doing it by telling the truth.

A story almost unknown to today's generation is about the blasting of the First World War myth that the German Gotha bomber was invincible. It deserves a place in our history books.

So does, of course, the heroic defence of its convoy by the converted liner H.M.S. *Jervis Bay* in the face of overwhelming shellfire from the German pocket battleship *Admiral Scheer* in the Second World War.

And the single-ship encounter between the H.M.S. *Shannon* and the U.S.S. *Chesapeake* in 1813 is included because it's a stirring bit of history. It taught the persevering British at long last that they could vanquish a warship manned by their American cousins; and it taught the confident Americans not to expect an automatic triumph. (A gala dinner, prepared in advance in Boston for the captured Royal Navy officers, became just tables of empty plates.)

But why include the story of a gutter fighter like Mysterious Billy Smith?

Well, if he butted and gouged and elbowed, that's how we brought him up in the city slums of that era. And it's something to reflect on that a Canadian boxer did become a world champion twice. He is nearly forgotten to human memory now.

And as for those further ghost stories –

Everywhere I go, it seems, I'm haunted by new (or hardly used) ghosts.

When I was shopping for furniture in a Saint John department store this year the salesman, Gerry Kupkee, asked, "Did you ever hear of a haunted clock?"

I'd heard of haunted ships in Bay Chaleur, a haunted mountain in northwest New Brunswick, a haunted island off Grand Manan in the south, but a haunted clock was something new.

The old clock was in his aunt's home at Queenstown – a hillside village that enjoys one of the loveliest views of the St. John River, where picturesque green fingers of intervale land stretch far into the stream.

Nobody had wound the clock for years. It dozed peacefully silent on the mantel, just an ornament, a family heirloom.

One night, inexplicably, it gonged.

The next day the grandmother died.

People remarked on the strange coincidence; it became a conversation topic for a few days.

"A while later the clock unexpectedly struck the hour again," recalls Kupkee, "and my aunt's brother died."

Now some relatives were feeling uneasy. They assured each other that double coincidences occasionally do happen.

But the old clock had yet another gloomy prophecy in its works.

"It gonged again one evening," says Kupkee, frowning, "and by the next day my aunt's brother-in-law was dead."

What could the hapless family do?

It was easy.

Gerry Kupkee's cousin, then a teen-ager, cut off the old clock's striker and threw it away.

"That's enough out of you," he said firmly.

He not only removed the striker but also, apparently, exorcised the hex.

Peace – and good health – have reigned since.

Laugh Me Up Some More of Those Funny Names

No self-respecting book about New Brunswick should be published without Professor James DeMille's famous century-old poem about Indian place names, especially those two gentle St. John River tributaries the Skoodawabskooksis and Skoodawabskook. So here it is:

In New Brunswick We'll Find It

Sweet maiden of Passamaquoddy,
    Shall we seek for communion of souls
Where the deep Mississippi meanders,
    Or the distant Saskatchewan rolls?
Ah, no! in New Brunswick we'll find it,
    A sweetly sequestered nook –
Where the swift gliding Skoodawabskooksis
    Unites with the Skoodawabskook.

Meduxnekeag waters are bluer;
    Nepisiguit's pools are more black;
More green is the bright Oromocto,
    And browner the Petitcodiac;
But colours more radiant in autumn
    I see when I'm casting my hook
In the waves of the Skoodawabskooksis,
    Or perhaps in the Skoodawabskook.

Let others sing loudly of Saco,

Of Passadumkeag or Miscouche,
Of Kennebecasis or Quaco,
    Of Miramichi or Buctouche;
Or boast of the Tobique or Mispec,
    The Musquash or dark Memramcook;
There's none like the Skoodawabskooksis,
    Excepting the Skoodawabskook.

Think not, though the Magaguadavic
    Or Bocabec pleases the eye,
Though Chiputneticook is more lovely,
    That to either of these we will fly;
No, when in love's union we're plighted
    We'll build our log house by a brook
Which flows to the Skoodawabskooksis,
    Where it joins with the Skoodawabskook.

Then never of Waweig or Chamcook
    I'll think, having you in my arms;
We'll reck not of Digdeguash beauties,
    We'll care not for Pocologan's charms;
But as emblems of union forever,
    Upon two fair rivers we'll look;
While you'll be the Skoodawabskooksis,
    I'll be the Skoodawabskook.

Of course, any native-born New Brunswicker can reel off
these familiar names without even thinking – also Washa-
demoak, Pocowogamis, Mermerimammericook, Kouchiboug-
uac, Mogulaweechooacadie, and Keheequahauweekpahegan,
which of course was Big Beavers dam at the Reversing Falls.

But tourists for some reason find the old Maliseet and Micmac names hilarious. They ask New Brunswickers to keep saying them over and over, and they double up laughing every
time.

We can only envy these fortunate people who hail from
communities with sensible names easy to pronounce. Some of
their addresses in Canada, I noticed, were Horsefly and Ta Ta
Creek, B.C.; Dogpound, Alberta; Eyebrow and Moosejaw, Sas-

15

katchewan; Flin Flon, Manitoba; Wawa, Ontario; Louis de Ha Ha, Quebec; Ecum Secum, N.S.; Five Houses, P.E.I.; Cat Gut, Blow Me Down and Jerry's Nose, Newfoundland.

And the Americans! Why, one group of visitors from our good-neighbour country got a particularly hearty belly laugh out of native names because they themselves lived in apartment complexes and condominiums with distinguished titles like Sir Winston Churchill Heights, Royal Windsor Vista, Chesterfield Court.

Incidentally, their skyscraper apartments happened to be variously situated, they told us, on Snakeroot Road, Shot Town Road, Hardscrabble Road, at Yeehaw, Bowlegs Lake, Polecat Creek, and Ogeechee River. There were some Floridians among them who resided in condominiums near the Caloosahatchee River; or was it the Chattahoochee or the Chokoloskee? I can never remember; some of those foreign names are devilish hard to remember, let alone get your tongue around.

The visitors who laughed loudest at New Brunswick's Nepis-i-guit River, with the accent on the second syllable, and the old original name of Lorneville in the Saint John area – Pis-i-rin-co – came from the Buckingham Gardens Resort Colony in the U.S. South. Isn't that a lovely name? They mentioned that it's approximately between the Great Pee-Dee River and the Little Pee-Dee River, far from their former home on the Pisataqua River.

So, boys, let's whomp up some more of those funny names off the New Brunswick map and have another good guffaw.

Moral: Never Punch a Gentle Maritimer

The captain of the Ohio riverboat should have known better.

He had been puzzled over how to move a very heavy metal bell across the deck to make room for more freight.

Still pondering after dinner below with the passengers, he climbed back on deck – to find the bell was now on the other side of the ship.

"How did you do it?" he asked the deckhands in surprise.

With a laugh Tom Gardner, a newly hired crewman from New Brunswick, said, "I carried it over myself."

The other seamen chuckled to see a glowering cloud cross the skipper's face. Only moments before they had been astounded to watch the newcomer, a man nearing middle age, lift the bell and tote it across the deck.

The captain, a powerfully built figure, sized up the ordinary-looking crewman, and thundered: "Don't you get impertinent with me, mister!" He had seen no hint of the fact that this fellow was one of the strongest men in the world – that he had once carried a barrel of pork under each arm.

Earnestly Tom Gardner replied, "I only meant what I said."

Another few words exchanged – and the captain punched him in the face.

For one of the few times in Tom Gardner's life his cheeks flamed and his fury rose.

He retaliated with a mighty backhand blow, and the captain fell prone on the instant – dead.

Tom escaped to the west and was never heard from again.

So goes the legend – or part-legend – penned by contemporaries of Tom Gardner on the St. John River. Completely true or not, it illustrates two characteristics in the lives of Maritime Provinces strong men.

First, they were not all super-giants in stature. Tom Gardner, born in 1797 of United Empire Loyalist parents on the St. John River one mile above the Mactaquac branch, measured five feet ten and one-half inches in height and weighed only 175 pounds.

And secondly, matter not how gentle and soft-spoken they were, whenever they demonstrated their prowess there was always someone eager to pick a fight or challenge them to a trial of strength.

In York County, N.B., where Tom grew up to be a farmer and skilful boatman and streamdriver, he was known also as an unbeatable wrestler.

This reputation only spelled trouble. As a youth he was about to spend the night at Merritt's Hotel in Indiantown, Saint John, when Larry Stivers, a gambling swell, urged him to match grips with a champion wrestler named Wescott.

"He's bragging out there in the barroom," said Stivers. "I bet him fifty dollars I could find a twenty-year-old who could put him down."

Wescott was over six feet tall and tipped the scales at 200 pounds. Almost at the moment they tangled in the ring, Wescott's experience told: Tom Gardner found himself on his knees, with the champion's backers jeeringly giving him a hurrah.

This at last incensed Tom's good nature. With a great heave he rose to his feet and threw off his opponent. Then he grasped Wescott and whirled him head over heels and slammed him to the floor, where he lay gulping and helpless for several minutes. In fact, the old tales say, the champ never entered a ring again.

Merritt's Hotel was left with a souvenir seen by thousands of people in subsequent years: two gouge-marks on the low ceiling of the barroom, made by the champ's heels as he flew through the air.

In Fredericton the proprietor of the Golden Ball sent for Tom Gardner to help solve a chronic problem: an overbearing character named McGrath kept coming into the barroom and demanding that patrons treat him or be knocked flat.

Just to show what usually happened, the proprietor, a Mr. Avery, took Tom up to the bar counter and said aloud, "I'll treat you. What is your pleasure?"

Tom was about to lift the filled glass when it was snatched away. "McGrath is the name," said the fiery-eyed newcomer; "after me is manners," and poured it down his gullet.

This was an easy one. Tom simply took him by the neck and flung him out through the swinging doors, where he landed bruised and cut on the sidewalk. He never came back to the Golden Ball.

Word spread widely about the fabulous deeds of the strong man. Once a gang of workers was about to move a huge length of timber; no single lumberjack was able to lift it more than two inches. Tom Gardner asked four men to sit on it. And then he hoisted the big timber – and the four men – so high they leaped off in fear. On another occasion, with only one hand gripping the rung of a chair, he lifted the chair and a 200-pound man sitting on it. In a wrestling bout he soon pinned the European champion who had challenged him.

Whence did Tom inherit his tremendous strength? That's an intriguing point. Not from his father, who was just a medium-sized farmer of unprepossessing build, but from his mother, who was a big brawny woman with muscular arms.

And oddly, although Tom's two brothers were more like their father, his sister resembled her mother.

It happened that one day a renowned wrestler arrived from the Miramichi River country to challenge this Tom Gardner he'd heard so much about.

"He's not home," said the sister, "but I'll have a go with you." And to his stunned surprise she threw him three times.

The visitor didn't come back for a test with her big brother.

By chance I heard that Dr. Carey K. Ganong, professor emeritus of law at Purdue University, Lafayette, Indiana, and formerly professor of economics at several U.S. centres of learning, was an authority on Tom Gardner, so I got in touch with him.

Born at Advocate Harbour, N.S., in 1894, Dr. Ganong in infancy moved with his family to Saint John, and later spent several years in the Belleisle Bay area, leaving at age sixteen to begin his career as a Western Union Telegraph operator.

This distinguished retired educator – a tall, well-built man with grey hair, mustache and trimmed beard – was still active as ever in his mid-eighties. He was residing in Orange City, Florida, and making occasional trips north to revisit familiar haunts in the St. John River country.

Fascinated by the tales he heard as a boy about the phenomenal strong man, Carey Ganong took a renewed interest when his widowed mother in 1916 married Chipman Gardner Colwell, a grandson.

Dr. Ganong told me Tom Gardner was remembered as a good-looking, curly-haired young man with a well-muscled body – "like a Greek god" – and amiable and modest in personality.

But he had two extraordinary physical attributes:

"All his teeth were molars," Dr. Ganong said. "And his ribs were indistinguishable. That is to say, either Nature had used bone-plates for ribs, or his ribs were concealed by his muscular development."

And what muscular development! There was the time two crews of lumberjacks, one from Maine and the other from New Brunswick, thought up a novel contest after delivering their rafted logs to sawmills at the mouth of the St. John River: Which side had the stronger leader?

The test weight was a timber thirty feet long, two feet in diameter at the butt.

Each boss managed to lift the butt end without difficulty.

Each then lifted it with a man sitting astride the butt.

The Maine captain grunted and groaned at the next test – but couldn't budge the log with two men aboard.

"Now all of you Yankees get on the log," Tom Gardner said.

The whole crew obliged – and Tom Gardner hoisted the butt end to his chin and let it fall.

And there was the time at Jemseg Creek, off the St. John River, when construction of a schooner was halted because heavy rains had turned the ground into a morass. Even a team of oxen, floundering in the mud, couldn't manoeuvre the mast up to be swung over to the hull. Tom Gardner came along and, eyewitnesses said, raised the heavy end of the mast out of the mire and tossed it like a caber up on to the deck.

Dr. Ganong heard countless other instances of the man's unbelievable strength from his step-father and old river residents – as when Tom Gardner juggled three 32-pound shots in his hands as deftly as if they were oranges . . . when he picked up a 1,200-pound anchor by its flukes and walked around with it . . . when he toted two 200-pound barrels of flour – one under each arm – through waist-high snow that average men couldn't struggle through with their arms empty.

Dr. Ganong heard, too, the oft-told tale about Tom Gardner's powerful sister – but with a slightly different ending. The wrestling challenger apparently wasn't thrown three times – he wasn't that lucky. Instead, on shaking hands with her as a preliminary courtesy, he fell to his knees and doubled up in anguish as her viselike grip crunched his fingers. It must be said for him that before he hastily took his leave, he remembered to thank her.

As far as Dr. Ganong could ascertain, Tom Gardner decided of his own volition to leave his homeland because of two tragedies he inadvertently caused.

The first occurred when, goaded into a fist fight, he hit his adversary with one smashing hay-maker that killed him.

Next came a rough-and-ready lumberjack who ceaselessly ridiculed Tom, castigating him as a coward if he wouldn't put up his fists. The drunker the challenger got, the more insulting he became, egged on by the hoots of woodsmen who wanted to see blood spilled. Tom Gardner kept demurring – until the tormentor slapped his face.

As had happened before, the enraged victim unleashed a shattering punch – and his assailant died instantly.

Many people down through the years have taken for granted that Tom Gardner fled New Brunswick because he feared the law would apprehend him. But Dr. Ganong points out this would be entirely out of character for such a conscientious fellow. Besides, killing a man in a provoked fight was not regarded in that era in quite the same serious light as it is today; common people duelled with their fists, gentlemen with pistols, and public opinion tended to be tolerant.

Probably – as Tom Gardner's grandson always believed – the memory of the two dead men was such a burden on his mind that he wanted to leave his old life behind and start anew. His wife had died, and after making arrangements for their little daughter Elizabeth to be well brought up, Tom bade the St. John River good-bye in 1837.

He was next heard of, Dr. Ganong recalls, working as a hand on an Ohio riverboat. It was there that Tom Gardner performed the incredible dinnertime feat of moving a 1,600-pound bell that had defied the crew's most strenuous efforts. And it was there he responded to the cynical captain's abusive taunts by back-handing him across the face, killing him on the spot.

"Hearing nothing from her father after the Ohio River incident, Tom Gardner's daughter Elizabeth assumed he had been arrested and hanged," Dr. Ganong says, "and her descendants agreed with her."

But Dr. Ganong, whose interest in the mysterious story had now become a hobby, disagreed. If the strong man was executed, he reasoned, surely someone at home would have heard. He felt a persistent hunch – a premonition perhaps – that eventually he would learn the last chapter.

And he did, in an unexpected way.

In 1941, after seeing a *Reader's Digest* article, "Do Your Eyes See Alike?" he went to the Dartmouth Eye Institute in Hanover, New Hampshire. His suspicion that he had aniseikonia – a sort of double vision – was confirmed.

After his return to Purdue, Dr. Ganong and his wife one day were visiting Mr. and Mrs. Harry Short in West Lafayette. Dr. Ganong told them about his eye trouble, describing it as essentially a physical peculiarity.

"Speaking of physical peculiarities," remarked his host, "my great-aunt married a man with the strangest I've ever heard of – all his teeth were molars."

Electrified, Dr. Ganong exclaimed, "Was that man's name Tom Gardner?"

"It was – but how on earth did you know?"

So Harry Short, a student of Mississipi River history, filled in the final chapter.

From the Ohio, Tom Gardner had found his way to the upper Mississippi, settling in Lansing, Iowa. There he married Harry Short's great-aunt, and became a partner in operating the family's steamboat business. The vessel *Lizzie Gardner* was nostalgically named, it seems, after Tom's daughter Elizabeth by his first marriage.

Evidently here Tom Gardner found the new existence his conscience had sought. He used his own name, which indicated he did not dread any retribution from the law. He lived as a well-to-do and well-liked businessman to the end of his days in 1872.

And there is no hint that any of his fellow citizens were ever aware of his fame as an incredibly strong man – a fame that had brought him only grief.

In southwestern New Brunswick old-timers still recall with awe the weight-lifting feats of William Rideout, a black-whiskered woodsman of peaceable nature who never tried to exploit his own strength. He stood more than six feet tall and weighed 220 pounds.

It was nothing for him to converse with a neighbour for a quarter of an hour while holding a 200-pound cask on one shoulder and 100-pound bag of meal under the other arm, and then climb over a five-bar fence rather than bother removing and replacing the cross-poles.

A worker at his farm in Oak Hill, Charlotte County, faced with the task of hitching the horse to "twitch" a massive timber to the back of the barn, was astonished to return after supper and find the boss walking around the barn with the pine timber balanced lightly on his shoulder.

Unhappily for William Rideout, like all reputably strong men (and also like reputably weak men), he was picked on.

In a woods camp, eight strapping lumberjacks ganged up on the big man and pummelled him down to the floor.

When several of his friends tried to intercede, Rideout waved them off.

"Thanks," he gasped, "but I'm coming right up."

He staggered to his feet, spinning off his attackers left and right, then proceeded to send them crashing down like pine trees, one by one.

William Rideout's fame, to his dismay, followed him like a malevolent shadow when he moved over the border to Lincoln, Maine.

In that community lived a great boastful lumberjack who told everyone he was looking forward to mixing it with this Canadian if they ever met.

When they did, the Maine man deliberately belittled Rideout to his face and invited him to fight.

The battle lasted about two seconds. Only one punch was banged home – by Rideout. The Maine lumberjack was out cold for half an hour.

The modest lettering on the headstone says:

Erected
To the memory of
Angus MacAskill
The Nova Scotia Giant
Who Died August 8, 1863
Aged 38 years

This simple tribute at Englishtown, Cape Breton, doesn't mention that MacAskill was believed to be the strongest man in the world in his time – possibly, some say, the most powerful human in history.

He was a real giant, as men grow – seven feet nine inches tall, weighing a hearty 425 pounds (and, as his admirers claimed, not an ounce of fat).

Any ordinary boy apparently can hope, if he wishes, that he may develop into another Cape Breton Giant, for Angus was just another normal-sized youngster until he reached his sixteenth birthday. Then he began to soar; at seventeen he was six feet seven inches, and counting.

His phenomenal strength was first demonstrated when his father and older brothers returning to the sawmill from dinner found fourteen-year-old Angus seated astride a heavy log on the ground – the same huge stick of timber that had been left reposing on the top of the sawpit, placed there by the grunting efforts of three able millhands. When Angus saw them coming he knew his rest period was over – so he simply lifted his tremendous timber bench and tossed it back up on the sawpit.

They tell of the time in a New York tavern he picked up a 140-gallon puncheon and, tilting it, swigged rum from the bung-hole . . . the time he lifted a 2,200-pound anchor over his head . . . the time he took the place of an ailing horse in a double team and easily helped the farmer finish his ploughing.

Hundreds of thousands of North Americans in countless cities and towns gasped with awe during the next five years to see Giant MacAskill clomping out on the stage in gargantuan boots beside his partner, the famous tiny General Tom Thumb. The grand climax came when the miniature man danced on the giant's hand.

(This act, an inspiration of fabulous showman P.T. Barnum, was also acclaimed in Europe. But Barnum had resorted to a bit of artistic licence in ballyhooing his fellow Connecticut native Tom Thumb, this midget whose real name was Charles Sherwood Stratton. When Tom was first exhibited he was only six years old, but he was so maturely built that Barnum presented him as a full-grown man – a man twenty-five inches tall and weighing fifteen pounds. In adulthood Tom Thumb was to grow up to be forty inches tall and weigh seventy pounds, which didn't make nearly so startling a contrast.)

In later years the busy Giant MacAskill gladly came back from the bright lights to his leisurely Nova Scotia home village of Englishtown, where he operated a store and two grist-mills.

But even he, towering figure though he was, couldn't be immune to the needling of challengers. He tried to ignore the taunts of a 250-pound boxer, but angrily agreed to meet him after his tormenter charged he was a coward.

The prospect of an epic battle attracted big-time gamblers and big-time money from many parts of Canada and the United States. Englishtown swarmed with visitors, all following the shrill pipes and booming drums of a kiltie band toward the converted barn that was to be the scene of decision.

The bare-knuckle fight, for shortness of duration, deserved a place in the *Guinness Book of World Records*. It was over before it began.

After the referee reminded them in centre ring about the rules, he ordered, "Now, shake hands."

They did – and a scream of anguish went up from the boxer. He collapsed to the floor. His hand looked as if it had been run through a grinding machine. It was a limp, useless mash of broken bones and bleeding flesh.

Phineas T. Barnum, that shrewd circus impressario, could have been forgiven if he wondered what super-vitamins they were feeding young Nova Scotians on these days.

After he had cashed in on Giant MacAskill at home and abroad, he found a new gold-mine in New Annan, Colchester County, N.S. – Giantess Anna Swan, born in 1846, who stood exactly as tall as the Cape Breton giant (seven feet, nine inches) and, when she doffed her voluminous clothes and her thirteen-button boots, weighed only five pounds less, at 420.

Instead of exhibiting her with a midget for contrast, he promoted a marriage between Anna and the "Kentucky Giant," Colonel Martin Van Buren Bates. Together they appeared before the crowned heads of Europe, dwarfing everyone they met, including the clergyman who wedded them in London and who kept looking Heavenward throughout the ceremony–not out of devoutness but to see the faces of the happy couple.

Was Benedict Arnold Misjudged?

Will the world's best-known traitor be rehabilitated some day?

If not vindicated, will Benedict Arnold at least win due recognition for his military accomplishments?

It's possible.

Several mysteries overhang the ill-starred career of this notorious figure who spent six years in New Brunswick among the displaced Tories after the U.S. Revolutionary War, yet was despised almost as much by his fellow United Empire Loyalists as by the Americans.

He was vain, imperious, and arrogant, contemporaries said. But so were many more recent military leaders, as we know, and they retained a devoted public following.

So it could not have been merely General Arnold's knack of riling people, of making them bristle at his overbearing manner.

The real reason was probably threefold. One was that a traitor often is unloved by anyone, even by the people who welcome his defection. That may account for the coolly formal and sometimes even hostile greeting accorded Arnold after the war in London, where he had expected something like a hero's welcome. Instead he was repeatedly snubbed. He was hissed when he went to a play with his pretty and loyal wife, the former Peggy Shippen of Philadelphia, who was twenty-two years his junior.

It should be noted, too, that among many Britons there was

considerable sympathy for the American cause, just as there would have been a few years ago if Britain and a rebellious Rhodesia had gone to war, for it wasn't a conflict between the Britain and the United States of today, but between the Mother Country and a colonial land peopled by generations of her own stock – practically a civil war.

The New Brunswick Loyalists' animosity towards General Arnold was aggravated by his reputation as a scheming double-crosser. In Saint John he had shipping interests, a timber log pond, also a store and warehouse, and he owned properties in Fredericton. When fire demolished his store in 1788, a former partner, Munson Hoyt, accused him of burning the building for the heavy insurance.

This touched off one of the bitterest legal altercations in the province's history. Each angry man sued the other. Hoyt became almost apoplectic with rage whenever he talked of Benedict Arnold, which was practically all the time, branding him "the greatest rascal that ever was" and accusing his erstwhile partner of bilking him of £700.

Just as infuriated, Arnold denounced Hoyt's charges as vicious absurd lies. He had been away at the time of the fire himself but his sons Richard and Henry were in the store when the fire erupted, Henry narrowly escaping death. Arnold fumed at the cruel absurdity of anyone's implying that a father deliberately risked his sons' lives for illegal gain. Further he contended Hoyt still owed him £2,000, and displayed promissory notes to back his claim.

Confidently Arnold launched a $5,000* action for defamation of character – an unimpressed jury awarded him a scant 20 shillings, which was worse than nothing.

His gnawing humiliation was not salved when a mob burned him in effigy – a dummy placarded "Traitor" – outside his home, keeping up a cacophony of raucous shouts and catcalls until the riot act was read and troops herded everyone homeward.

---

*In early colonial days New Brunswick used British pounds, American dollars, and other currencies at set rates of exchange.

Why did his neighbours detest Arnold?

As an instance, they asserted he had put over a typical fast deal on Nehemiah Beckwith, who was building a schooner for him on the St. John River. Arnold, the story goes, insisted on so many design changes as the job went along that Beckwith couldn't finish it within the contract time and had to forfeit so much cash as a penalty that he went bankrupt.

Benedict Arnold and his wife departed in 1791, resided for a while in the West Indies, then moved back to England. There he corresponded occasionally with the few sympathetic old friends he could count among the prominent Loyalist bigwigs in New Brunswick.

The ladies of Saint John society – and the gentlemen – genuinely missed Peggy Arnold, for wherever she travelled she had been as popular as her husband was disliked.

New Brunswick was left with varied mementos of the controversial general. His will is still formally registered. The documents of his property transfers still occupy their niche in the New Brunswick Museum archives. Many dignified old homes still have pieces of his mahogany furniture, bought at auction. From a viewing platform near the President Franklin D. Roosevelt summer home on Campobello Island you can see little Treat Island, now forlorn and forested, where Benedict Arnold stopped for groceries when he loaded timber ships in Passamaquoddy Bay; the reason for shopping at a store in such an isolated place was that the sea was the highway in that early era; there were practically no roads ashore.

Once when sailing the Passamaquoddy waters Benedict Arnold invited Colonel Crane of Eastport, Maine, to dine aboard his vessel. The Colonel, a revolutionary war veteran wounded at the siege of New York, retorted angrily:

"Before I would dine with that traitor, I would run my sword through his body."

Not everyone felt that bitter.

Another American veteran, Captain John Shackford of Newburyport, Massachusetts, who loaded ships under the supervision of Benedict Arnold at Campobello, said:

"I did not make myself known to him but frequently, as I sat upon the ship's deck, watched the movements of my old commander who had carried us through everything, and for whose skill and courage I retained my former admiration, despite his treason.

"But when I thought of what he had been and the despised man he then was, tears would come and I could not help it."

There appears to be a slow swing in the United States these days towards Captain Shackford's less-violent attitude, in the interest of historical integrity, now that passions have had nearly two centuries to cool.

One symptom came to light in recent years when history buff Vincent Lindner of Scotch Plains, N.J., persuaded a U.S. Army review board to agree to look into Benedict Arnold's 1779 conviction on two minor charges of misconduct for "using a public wagon to transport private property" – if the pertinent records were still available.

According to Lindner, a congressional committee vindicated Arnold on those charges at the time, but later an army court-martial convicted him on the same charges, which brought up the question of double jeopardy.

Will any of the tarnish ever be removed, however, from the abortive attempt by George Washington's trusted, "judicious and brave" general to hand over strategic West Point to the British?

Even that is possible, if remotely.

Arnold's modern-day proponents make these points:

The "great turncoat" is a misnomer. He had first turned traitor to the British flag, just as so many of his countrymen did. When he reverted to the British cause, he simply revoked his original act of treason; they didn't.

His behaviour may not have been basely motivated by the prospect of receiving £20,000 as a thank-you from the British, plus a commission as a brigadier-general in the British Army, as many critics have inferred.

Nor was it necessarily due to his jealousy over the acclaim other American officers were getting that he knew he himself deserved – for instance after the Second Battle of Saratoga, which historians say would have been a British victory if it had not been for Arnold's brilliant leadership of the American forces.

He may have been swayed, instead, by the hope that the United States would soon negotiate a peace – a goal the 1779 Continental Congress had approved – rather than become an independent nation under the possible domination of France. If such a rapprochement had been worked out, and the United States had been accorded a substantial new degree of autonomy while still retaining its ties with Britain, Benedict Arnold might have gone down in his country's annals as an historic peacemaker rather than a scoundrel.

His apologists emphasize that the general's courage was unquestioned. He could face anything with cool resolve, whether it be a man-to-man pistol duel or a crucial battle. He could ignore the painful nuisance of two leg wounds gouged by British gunfire at Quebec and Saratoga. After he returned to the British side, he distinguished himself as a leader in the New England and Virginia campaigns, apparently oblivious of the fact that capture would mean instant execution. In fact, he escaped several times from skilfully organized American manoeuvres to trap him personally.

But perhaps the most persuasive American talking-point on Benedict Arnold's behalf is, paradoxically, that without him there might be no United States today.

This is because his very successful harassing attacks against the British fleet on Lake Champlain gave General Washington's war-weary forces priceless extra months to recover, regroup, and reorganize for the next year's campaign.

The Baby Needed Four Storks

"Paul Bunyan was a giant of a man," the lady with the lively twinkle in her eyes was saying, "so he was a pretty big baby when he was born.

"The legend is it took four storks to carry him, but the storks got tired out and had to come down for a rest. The baby walked the last half-mile himself."

She laughed, for she had an outgoing personality and took a real enjoyment in telling folklore stories, this historian who had invited my wife and myself in to talk about Acadian tales.

It was difficult to realize we were not in a home living room but in the reception room of the convent of the Order of the Assumption in Edmundston, N.B. – and our modernly dressed hostess with the merry smile and a natural strawberry blonde complexion was a nun, Sister Catherine Jolicoeur, a lecturer at the St. Louis-Maillet University Centre.

It was difficult because in growing up I had a fixed mental image of nuns as serious, expressionless people of a different world, or at least out of this one, with flowing black skirts sweeping the ground, metal-rimmed glasses and faces as white as flour, which came not only from ascetic living but also the fact that the pleated white coif shielded them from sun and wind and from seeing mankind's seamier behaviour.

I'd gone to the pulpmill city of Edmundston in the Madawaska County panhandle of New Brunswick – the storied "Republic of Madawaska" – to try to track down age-old reports that fabulous lumberjack Paul Bunyan was born somewhere up there, contrary to the strident claims made by other provinces and states all the way out to the Pacific coast.

The Republic of Madawaska, bordering both Maine and Quebec, is unique in all of Canada. It's a hospitable, ebullient, blithely happy, music-loving land, mainly French-speaking, but probably the most bilingual part of New Brunswick – a meld of four influences: Acadian French, Quebec French, English New Brunswick, and American. Madawaska was first called a "republic" in derision long years ago when its carefree inhabitants became notorious for ignoring provincial regulations about such minor things as Sunday bars, movies, and sports.

Accepting the criticism as a compliment, the people adopted their own coat-of-arms – a fiery torch with a handshake underneath – and amid due ceremony granted honorary citizenship in the republic to distinguished visitors. Thus Madawaska developed its own brand of separatism – if whimsical and benign – long before anyone heard of the Parti Québécois.

An hour before, I had climbed the long flights of steps to the sprawling University Centre. The staff obligingly tried in their best English to help me, but finally shook their heads and said, "If only Sister Jolicoeur were here."

The name struck a memory chord. Could this be the same Sister Jolicoeur, originally from Quebec's Gaspé coast, who had made a lifetime hobby of collecting sightings of flaming phantom ships in Bay of Chaleur and around the world? Yes, they said excitedly. I had talked with her on the phone when she was teaching school at the little northern New Brunswick meat-packing village of Paquetville two years before. At that time she had records of 1,070 sightings of ghost ships.

When we went to the convent and luckily found her in, I asked, "Have you added to those 1,070 sightings?" Hers was a smile of achievement. "I have 2,034 – nearly a thousand more. One was on New Brunswick's east coast at Shediac in 1976; people reported seeing a ship on fire out in the bay, but by the time the Mounties got there it was gone." Now, she

33

added, she's gathering material also on Acadian folklore and traditions.

Then what about Paul Bunyan? Was he actually a French Canadian? Was he born in the Republic of Madawaska, not in Quebec, Nova Scotia, Ontario, Maine, Minnesota, Wisconsin, Michigan, Oregon, Washington, or the countless other areas that have staked rights to him as a native son?

Sister Jolicoeur replied with a shrug, "Everybody wants Paul Bunyan. Even a commentator in France said he was simply a distortion of Napoleon. A Russian called him Paul Bunyanski."

"What's your own opinion?"

"It's possible," she said, "that Paul Bunyan isn't a true legendary figure at all, but a myth started by the lumber companies early in this century for the entertainment of the woodsmen – or even as an incentive."

Certainly, as an example to work harder, Paul Bunyan couldn't have been bettered. He was far more than the Six Million Dollar Man of his day – he was at least a Hundred Million. You've heard that the world's highest tides rise and fall fifty-three feet in the Bay of Fundy? Ever know why? It was started simply by the rocking of his cradle. Many people say he was born on the shore of the forty-mile-wide salt-water expanse that separates New Brunswick and Nova Scotia.

As a youth of herculean proportions, Paul could swing his scythe and strip a whole hillside of hay in one blow. Just one swipe at a tall pine and he yelled, "Timber!"

Talk about Seven League Boots – he traversed New Brunswick in just seven strides. He often went to the Maritime seaside for a dip, because he contended Lake Superior was too cramped for his size.

As Paul Bunyan grew bigger, Sister Jolicoeur's notes went on, the yarns grew too. Lumbercamp story-spinners said he invented stream-driving and saw-logging, also the double-bitted axe. That's what cleared New Brunswick forests of the prolific ironwood trees, which were reputedly so hard that woodsmen's axes bounced off them. Paul Bunyan devised a method of slicing into one trunk, then cleaving another on the back-swing.

(Another version says he put his loggers on a turntable, so they could whack a tree first from one side, then the other.)

Around him gathered a host of characters equally fabulous. There was Babe, the little ox he found frozen in the Michigan snow; but Babe, though always afterward blue, grew mightily too, measuring forty-two axe-handles and two plugs of chewing tobacco across his horns. Others were Big Swede, the logging foreman, and the bookkeeper, Johnny Inkslinger, who incidentally invented the fountain pen when he coupled a fire hose to a fifty-gallon hogshead of water on an outdoor carrier. Ole the blacksmith could almost challenge Paul Bunyan himself; he could lift one of Babe's huge iron shoes off the ground (though to accomplish this he sank down almost to his hips in the hard rock). And Paul's chief cook, Hot Biscuit Joe – believe it or not, he had sixteen assistant cooks with sides of bacon laced around their feet so they could skate all over the huge shallow griddles and keep the stove well lubricated for flapjack-frying.

According to such folktales they tell in the deep timberland of New Brunswick, Paul Bunyan and his entourage stayed in the province "from the Summer of the Blue Snow to the Year the Rain Came Up From China" – if you can figure out that one. They cut timber on the Big Onion River and the Little Garlic that flows into it. And when the smell blinded the whole crew, Paul Bunyan was equal to the occasion. He merely invented the gas mask, also the lasso axe (which enabled a lumberjack to stand far away and do his chopping with a forty-fathom rope).

Absolutely nothing, in fact, fazed our hero. When he rafted so many logs to the mouth of the St. John River that they jammed the entire harbour, the avaricious consignees thought up a technicality – they would refuse to accept the logs, hoping they could force him to sell on their terms.

Undaunted, Paul Bunyan fed his ox Babe sixteen barrels of salt, led him down to Fredericton, seventy miles from Saint John, and said, "Drink up."

A few swallows later, the river level went down, the logs floated back up to Grand Lake and were safely corralled in booms. This was why, in case you didn't know, the river now flows alternately upward and downward at Saint John. This was how the famed Reversing Falls were born.

When he eventually hiked away from New Brunswick, Paul Bunyan's mammoth shoes were following in the footsteps of thousands of lumberjacks who left for the more adventurous life, taller trees, fatter pay envelopes of the West: unique characters like Bill Fahey, from Kent County, a lumberman who never encountered another man as far as the Pacific coast who could floor him in a fist fight. In their trail they left little touches of New Brunswick – like the appellation "the Main John" for the boss man. It originally denoted John Glasier of Sunbury County, one of New Brunswick's first senators after Confederation, better remembered as the first lumber boss to drive logs over the brink of Grand Falls, which is among the largest waterfalls of Eastern North America.

Paul Bunyan's feats seemingly became more spectacular, more awe-inspiring, the farther west he went. In Ontario they say the smokestacks of his sawmills were hinged about halfway down so they could be collapsed to let the sun and the moon go by. He trekked past New York and Pennsylvania – and the deep footprints in his wake filled with water and became the Great Lakes.

He really did a job on the Prairies and the U.S. Mid West. He methodically sheared them of trees; then he and the Big Swede and Johnny Inkslinger lifted the landscape and turned it upside down, thus burying the stumps to cultivate the ground for grain-growing.

In Wisconsin Paul Bunyan built such a vast logging camp, so they said, the waiters had to wear roller skates to tend the five-mile-long tables. He chopped down all of North Dakota's trees in a month. He did the same for Nevada (and on the way left the dragging trail of his gigantic axe behind, thus creating the Grand Canyon).

Is there any element of truth in the Paul Bunyan story?

Some old-time New Brunswickers, who lived more than fifty years ago, contended there really was a Paul Bunyan, a big French Canadian born a century before around the headwaters of the 450-mile-long St. John River. Tales of his prodigious strength, told and retold by admirers and cynically magnified by detractors, grew and expanded until a king-sized legend was born.

Others, leaning toward Sister Jolicoeur's suggestion, maintained that the first public mention of Paul Bunyan appeared in a Detroit newspaper in 1909, merely the figment of a feature writer's imagination.

But in the 1950's, when the Forest Products History Foundation of St. Paul, Minnesota, tried to pin down the answer to the mystery, a veteran Ontario woods worker told the foundation's research seminar in Fort Francis, Ontario: "The superdeeds of Paul Bunyan were being told around Ontario lumber camps when I started in 1889."

Did he know who the original Paul Bunyan was? "I only know," said the lumberjack, Bob Mitchell, "everyone said he was a huge Canadian who emigrated to the United States to work in the big timber."

Whatever the truth may be, the silliest idea was voiced by a man who told me, "He must have been born in Maine – they have a monument to him in Bangor."

That doesn't prove Paul Bunyan was born in Maine any more than London Bridge proves the Arizona desert is England, the liner *Queen Mary* proves that Long Beach, California, is Southampton, or the presence of the H.M.S. *Bounty* reproduction proves that St. Petersburg, Florida, is Liverpool.

It only proves that the people of Maine, like all Americans, are very imaginative and aggressive tourist promoters.

Artful Dodgers
on the Border

With horses galloping, the truck wagon clattered across the international bridge from Calais, Maine, to St. Stephen, N.B.

"Can't wait!" the driver shouted to the Canadian customs officer. "Got to get my brother to hospital quick. He's had a fit!"

Sure enough, the brother was stretched out on a leather couch inside the wagon. There was no hospital on the Calais side.

"Go ahead," the customs man waved him on.

Why did the victim take a fit? The answer is simple. Indeed, the customs officers may well have suspected it – because, says retired Customs Inspector Kenneth Webber of St. Stephen, the boys develop a sixth sense for spotting a phony.

The Canadian driver of the wagon had just won a contest for collecting Larkin's Soap coupons. But the prize, a leather couch, was delivered to a warehouse on the Maine side of the boundary, separated by the narrow St. Croix River from New Brunswick.

So the winner used his ingenuity to try to outwit customs. This was a popular pastime on the border in those days; everyone thought that eluding the customs was a healthful recreation, a challenge to adroitness, a privilege probably embodied in the Bill of Rights, and morality had nothing to do with it.

Smuggling stories kept bobbing up all through my half-century of newspaper work, because New Brunswick happens to be the only one of four Atlantic Provinces that has a land border with the United States.

This proximity led to bizarre situations in earlier times. When the boundary was..finally determined, some people found their houses astride the line; more than one couple slept with their heads in Canada and their feet in the United States. Many French pioneers along the Bay of Fundy who fled from the British in 1755 hewed out log houses in the northwest of Acadia – to discover later that they and their brothers and sisters were now variously Americans or Canadians, depending on where they built.

Enterprising merchants erected "line stores" on the exact boundary, so they could surreptitiously sell to both sides. It was more than the customs men could do to keep watch on them all. In the prohibition era, several line stores had portable bars.

"I remember a fellow named Jake had a bar like that on the Woodstock-Houlton road," retired Inspector Webber says with a nostalgic smile. "The bar could be wheeled across to the U.S. side when Canadian customs men approached, or vice versa from the U.S. to the Canadian side. Either way, the customers took it in their stride, trotting along right behind the bar."

The line stores went out of business when Canada and the United States drew up an agreement that a ribbon of land should separate the two countries, and no one would be allowed to do business or build a home in that no man's land. Some opportunist owners of line stores sold their buildings to the Canadian government to use as customs stations.

But after all these years there are still numerous anomalies on the border. The Aroostook Valley Country Club at Four Falls, N.B., is so close to the line its parking lot and pro shop are on the American side at Fort Fairfield. The club uses two different phone services – the New Brunswick Telephone Company and the New England Telephone and Telegraph Company. Golfers joke that if you hook your drive on the first hole, you may hook it right out of Canada.

Along the boundary, restaurants have their special problems. At York's in Andover, proprietor Hubert St. Thomas must be ready to cope not only with both English and French languages but also with two currencies, two time zones, two nationalities of food inspectors, two ways of figuring distance and temperature now that Canada has gone metric. Fortunately, distance is often figured now in minutes or hours instead of miles or kilometers.

You overhear him saying on the phone: "Yes, madam, dinner for four. Where are you now? That's seventy-five minutes from here, so we'll say six-thirty – that's Canadian time – five-thirty your time. And we'll have a highchair ready."

Most international spot of all is Roosevelt Campobello International Park, a natural preserve of 2,800 acres on a New Brunswick fishing island. The island, a geographical anachronism situated only yards from Lubec, Maine, is fifty-five miles by highway from the New Brunswick mainland. It's a unique place, the site of the huge F.D.R. summer cottage and other homes of affluent New Yorkers from the 1880's on, and it's the only park in the world administered by two countries. The chairmanship of the commission has alternated back and forth, usually between Senator Edmond S. Muskie of Maine and Lieutenant-Governor Hedard J. Robichaud of New Brunswick. The policy is to keep a balance between Canadian and American park workers, and to see as far as possible that both receive commensurate social security and other benefits.

On Campobello, incidentally, the customs encountered a memorable case, one that shook even an experienced officer.

A Nova Scotia car drove over the bridge from Lubec and the Campobello officer said, "Anything to declare?"

"Nope," replied the young driver. "Nothing at all."

"Open the trunk, please."

The youth turned the key and lifted the trunk lid.

A white-haired old man was lying there jackknifed up, his knees to his chin.

"I thought," said the flabbergasted customs man, "you told me there was nothing in the trunk."

"Nope; I said we had nothing to declare."

"Then who's this?"

"It's only Grampa. He died two days ago in New Jersey, and

we're taking him back to Nova Scotia to bury him."

At St. Stephen, customs officer Webber also met with strange contraband.

An old Dodge car came across from the U.S. side, and Mr. Webber, alone on duty, signalled it to go ahead.

Ten minutes later the same car, with the same young man at the wheel, came over the bridge from the U.S. side again.

"I realized," said Officer Webber, "he had gone up a few miles to Milltown, and crossed back to Maine. The first time he wanted to see if I'd stop him. Now he was hoping to get through easily again."

"So I said, 'Open your trunk.' "

Inside, curled up, was a very worried Maine state senator, a married man who had been officially prohibited from coming into Canada because he was having an affair with a girl in New Brunswick. The girl similarly had been refused entry into the United States.

"You've no idea," recalls Mr. Webber, "of the resourcefulness of some people. Why, occasionally, this man would pay the boy to drive him to Robbinston, Maine, and take the ferry to St. Andrews, N.B., and then down here." He shook his head, "I guess love will find a way."

Shortly after this discovery the customs man was confronted by a furious enquirer – the wife of the state senator.

"Did you find my husband," she demanded, "in the trunk of a car? That's what I heard!"

Witnesses said Mr. Webber looked his pious best, rolled his eyes heavenward, and replied, "I found somebody's husband, madame, but I can't say whether it was yours or not."

Fortunately, most encounters were less of a strain on his discretion. Like the time he instinctively knew, as he saw a bulky woman walking over the old Union Bridge, what she was up to.

This was when you had to buy margarine in Canada in plain white, like lard. In the United States you could buy it not only more cheaply, but also in packaged quarter-pound yellow blocks.

Many St. Stephen women had tried to bring chilled American margarine across – with the small blocks stuffed in their girdles – so many, in fact, that this international span became known as the Margarine Bridge.

"Or maybe," the long-retired inspector reminisces, "they were more scared of the other fellows than me."

When the over-plump woman said she had nothing to declare, the customs man asked with concern, "You're sure you're not getting a touch of jaundice? You seem to be turning yellow."

"No, I'm fine," she replied, but she sounded anxious and was shifting from foot to foot.

He motioned her on, because keeping her talking would only involve two hazards: either her midriff would freeze, or the yellow margarine would melt and run down her legs.

Now, Ken Webber could be a hard-nosed official when he suspected people of flagrantly violating the law. He has Phil Silvers' knack of drawing himself up and righteously squinting down obliquely at wrong-doers through horn-rimmed spectacles, like an accusing wrath from on high; and this ability not only made him more fearsome at such times but also helped make him a hilarious after-dinner speaker, one of the most entertaining in Canada. After his retirement he was elected to the New Brunswick Legislature as a Liberal, and became minister of labour in the cabinet of Premier Louis J. Robichaud.

But he also had a heart – as many customs officers do, difficult as it may be for some travellers to believe.

There was the time two women, sisters, came walking over the Union Bridge wearing big black capes that bulged out all around their waists, especially in the rear.

"I knew what they were doing," Mr. Webber said with a sigh. "They'd been doing it all along. You see, in those early days all St. Stephen merchants had warehouses over on the Maine side, and the goods were smuggled across, usually by boat." He added that the old Union Bridge was not manned after midnight till morning, so undoubtedly a lot of merchandise was furtively moved over, under and around the barricades.

"These women had picked up goods in Calais, and I knew what – because they stuck out so far in the back you could hang your hat on it. It was rolls of wallpaper."

The customs officer let them go by. Next day he visited Calais, then came over the bridge and appeared at the ladies' front door.

One of the women answered the bell – and at the sight of the customs man with rolls of wallpaper under his arm she was so startled that, after devoutly looking skyward, she crossed herself and exclaimed: "Holy Mother!"

"I'm tired of seeing you and Sis coming over looking like the Riddle Rider" (a black-caped, black-sombreroed star in western movies of the day), said Mr. Webber. "So as soon as you order the paste, let me know and I'll bring it over too."

However, the narrow river itself, not the bridge, was the favourite route of smugglers. Anyone in St. Stephen will happily recount the tale of the man who one springtime, after the turn of the century, tried to bring a Big Chief furnace over into Canada in a small rowboat. Paddling among chunky ice cakes, he got panicky when the boat tipped – but it was too late to stop the furnace from toppling into the freezing waters.

Commented Ken Webber, "The St. Croix *Courier* printed an editorial commending him for his community spirit in trying to heat the river and keep it open."

And there was the father-and-son smuggling team who always brought rum across to Canada in a wash boiler. The boy rowed a boat across the river towing the floating tub by a rope, the other side of the tub being connected to a long rope held by his father on the American side. Whenever the boy suspected Canadian customs agents were near by, he shouted, "Pa!" and the long rope hauled the tub back to the Calais shore.

Customs men had to have good memories. A Canadian woman walking back home across the bridge pushing her baby in a shiny stroller would normally arouse no suspicion – not unless the officers happened to remember she went over to Calais an hour ago on a street car with the baby on her lap.

Sometimes they chanced on smuggling merely by saying pleasantries – like the rainy day Ken Webber spoke to a St. Stephen man returning afoot, huddled under his umbrella, with his brother following.

"Well," the customs man said congenially, "what's under the umbrella?"

This threw the man into a panic. Under stress he always used the expletive "jumped up." He exclaimed, "Jumped up! Jumped up! I've got one shoe, and Wilmot's coming up behind with the other." It was true: Each was holding up a shining new shoe under the ribs of the umbrella.

Undoubtedly the officers didn't always bear down as hard as they could. They spiced their sternness with a sense of humour – and human sympathy.

Often, Mr. Webber recalls, women would come over and announce straight-faced they had nothing to declare – "and the smell of coffee would knock you over."

Once a woman tried to get by with a smuggled American alarm clock hidden in her underclothes.

Either by unlucky mischance or through the mischievousness of a store clerk, the alarm was set for the moment the good lady was being interviewed by the Canadian customs. When it went off, she jumped a foot.

"Excuse me," the customs officer said gallantly. "Please go on – I must answer the telephone."

Ken Webber was a match in quick thinking.

"During the Depression," he said, "money was very hard to get on both sides of the border. Calais had a Five and Ten, but there was no store like that on the Canadian side. St. Stephen housewives would do anything to get their children a few cheap ten-cent toys for Christmas, so they were always coming back over the Union Bridge looking twice as fat as usual."

One day two women slowly plodded across the bridge. They were so loaded they had to walk splay-footed because they couldn't get their legs closer together.

"Have you anything to declare?" Mr. Webber asked.

"No, nothing," replied one woman.

The customs man noticed the laces were loose on one of her high fur-topped boots.

"You'd better fix your overshoe! Here, just put your foot up on this bench."

When a customs officer makes a helpful suggestion, people

are quick to comply. But when the woman put her foot on the bench and leaned over, a loud voice far inside her clothing shrilled:

"*Mama-a-a-a-a!*"

Mr. Webber waved down a passing taxi:

"Get this lady over to the Canadian side quick before something happens!"

One of the few persons who ever completely dumbfounded the Canadian customs was only a boy.

Every day he travelled the bridge from St. Stephen to Calais and back again. Sometimes he walked; sometimes he rode his bicycle. But always, without fail, he carried a big canvas bag of sand either over his shoulder or in the bicycle carrier basket.

Naturally the U.S. customs stopped him and asked what was in the bag.

"Nothing but sand," was the reply.

They made him spread it out all over the counter.

It contained nothing but sand.

Reluctantly they helped him load it back in the bag. The youth was compelled to undergo the same experience when he returned over the bridge to enter Canada. Once again: nothing.

This went on and on all summer and fall. Sometimes customs on either side would let him go by a dozen times, then pounce and insist the bag be emptied. Always, nothing.

Years later the boy, now grown up into his twenties, met a retired customs superintendent in St. Stephen.

"If you wouldn't mind," said the ex-official earnestly, "now that I'm no longer connected with the customs service, I don't want to go to my grave without knowing something. Please tell me. What were you smuggling?"

The young man replied, "Bicycles."

Glooscap:
He Was the Greatest

Did you ever wonder how the Petitcodiac tidal bore began rushing up the river from the Bay of Fundy?

The explanation was quite simple to the primitive Indians.

The dastardly monster Eel had muddied up the river and chased out the fresh fish. So hero-god Glooscap endowed Lobster with great size and strength to kill the troublemaker.

According to the Micmacs of Big Cove in Kent County, the great cresting, roaring wave thereafter became a twice-a-day replay of the epic turmoil in which Lobster vanquished Eel.

And the Reversing Falls at the narrow mouth of the St. John River – they were understandable, too.

Big Beaver had built a mischievous dam that backed up the swollen river waters far upstream, flooding the countryside. Glooscap smashed the barrier with his stone club.

One piece of the dam became lodged as Partridge Island at the entrance of Saint John harbour. Glooscap's broken club itself is now known as Split Rock, just below the Falls. The hero-god pursued and slew Big Beaver at his house on the Long Island opposite Rothesay in the wide Kennebecasis tributary, a place now called The Minister's Face.

One version says Glooscap killed some of the beaver family at Milkish bay on a white granite rock which still bears red stains. A lone member of Big Beaver's household escaped far up river. To try to head him off, the pursuing Glooscap hurled two huge stones, which were named by the Indians the "Tobique Rocks."

At Mactaquac Creek, where the going was arduous, Glooscap abandoned his snowshoes, which became islands too.

After demolishing a beaver dam at Grand Falls, he paddled his stone canoe (with a homemade stone paddle) back to Saint John. This overawed his people; they made him a chief.

The future of the liberated St. John River was debated at length by Glooscap and his brother. They finally decided – as a convenience to Indian paddlers – to let the tide run upstream to Springhill half the time, and downstream the other half. This was the origin of the two-way Reversing Falls.

In short, the imaginative powers of the Maliseets, Micmacs, Passamaquoddies, and Penobscots, all Algonquin tribes, were prodigious. They could romanticize and dramatize to explain away any natural phenomenon. Old chiefs can draw on their memories for countless legends of why things are as they are – how the rabbit lost his tail, why the tall pines whisper, why Turtle has black spots under his shell. This may surprise some white people who always thought of early Indians as obtuse, haughty, unfeeling, unflinching, stoic.

Glooscap was infinitely more powerful than any Paul Bunyan, for he was a deity as well as a super-brave. He could do anything. Like the legendary wood-chopper, he could leave his footprints as lakes, and blow out enemies' campfires with a single puff. But he could also transform huge animals into tiny creatures, and vice versa.

For example, when he asked a lion-sized squirrel what he would do if he met a human, the squirrel ran growling to a tree stump and ripped it apart with its teeth and claws.

"Glooscap," the Maliseet legend goes, "put his hand on the squirrel's back three times and thus reduced him to the stature he is now."

When Glooscap asked the same question of a bear, it ambled away a few steps and merely looked back over its shoulder at him. So Glooscap let it be.

Indians said the wild goose was Glooscap's camp guardian, the loon and the wolf his watchdogs. (The melancholy cries of the loons were a soulful call to their master; the loons previously had been dogs, but were turned into birds when Glooscap went away from his stone cave.)

Implicitly, too, the tribes believed Glooscap had arrived on the North American coast in his stone canoe (which became a vast granite island called Newfoundland).

He created people merely by shooting arrows into the trunks of ash trees; out stepped full-grown braves and squaws.

But Glooscap performed such miracles amidst difficulties. Hovering about him all the time were discordant influences – cannibal giants of stone and ice, witches and wizards, Little People, high-spirited jokers such as rabbits and otters and badgers, not to mention his brother Malsum, who possessed wicked powers.

A folktale recalls that while Glooscap was creating the forest animals by moulding them out of clay in his hands, one glob of clay slipped and fell when Malsum whispered malicious magic words. The peculiar animal thus born had the ability to become, at will, a beaver or a badger or a wolverine. Exclaimed Malsum: "His name shall be Lox!"

With a sigh Glooscap ordained, "Then allow Lox to reside amongst us in peace, if he will."

But Lox wouldn't. He began furtively agitating among the bigger animals, goading gigantic Moose into believing his antlers could hurl a man to the roof of the world.

When Moose asked Glooscap for a man to pitch skyward, the hero-god laid a hand on him – and Moose suddenly shrank to his present size.

Wherever you travel in the Maritimes, you'll hear Glooscap legends and see their symbolism.

For example, half a mile below Boar's Head near the St. John River outlet you may discern the form of a man's head – a head with curly hair – in the cliff.

This, an old Maliseet told historian Edward Jack, is Glooscap's image, for it was here that he arrived when he first paddled down the river to smash Big Beaver's dam.

As you leave Saint John and sail down the Bay of Fundy shoreline, you may see a place where Glooscap left his pack, between Manawagonish Island and the mouth of the Musquash.

When Glooscap returned to search for it, he discovered a sable chewing on the pack. The pack was transformed into a huge rock – with a hole which the sable is supposed to have gnawed.

"When I was a boy," the wrinkled old Indian told Mr. Jack, "we used to go down the river and on to Lepreau in our canoes for cranberries in the autumn, and when we were passing Glooscap's face and head we always threw tobacco into the water as an offering, so that we might have a calm time going and returning."

While living on the island of Grand Manan at the entrance to the Bay of Fundy, Glooscap heard that the great Indian Devil had been wreaking havoc on the New Brunswick mainland.

Immediately he bade goodbye to his grandmother, Noogumee, who was also his faithful housekeeper, and crossed over to Lepreau on the back of a whale (which will hardly seem improbable to youngsters who've seen a man travelling on the back of Shamu, the whale at Sea World in Florida).

At Long Reach on the St. John River, continues the legend, Glooscap reproached the Devil and ordered him: "Go away!" The Devil scornfully turned his back.

Glooscap could be a fierce man-god of action. He drew his stone tomahawk and, after a battle that made the ground quaver and filled the air with flying rocks, he smote off the Devil's head and threw it far away over the azure hills.

Even today it's seen near the St. Croix River as "the Devil's Head."

Unfortunately the Devil, it should be added, saved his own life by a magic charm, so he's still on the prowl.

A friendly rivalry has grown up between New Brunswick and Nova Scotia as to who really owns Glooscap. Actually, he left his deep imprint almost everywhere in the Maritime Provinces. Nova Scotians claim his permanent home was at Cape Blomidon, near Kentville and Wolfville, and they can even decipher his footprints on the red cliffs. From the nearby beaches he gathered amethysts which he made into jewelry for his devoted grandmother. (He never married.) The coastal highway from Cape Blomidon to Amherst has been named "the Glooscap Trail."

Prince Edward Islanders contend just as vehemently he made his summer home there.

New Brunswickers think of him endlessly paddling up and down the St. John River in his stone canoe, stopping at Maliseet encampments of conical bark-covered wigwams to teach handicrafts to the young, and tell them how to use herbs as medicines. Their legends tell of him returning home for a well-deserved rest, and, apparently as an early-day plastic surgeon, "renewing his grandmother's youth four times." The neighbours always knew when he was home, because outside he'd hang his tumpline – the rainbow – to show everyone all was well.

Surprisingly, Glooscap never looked older than thirty, Indian legends said.

What happened to him?

This invincible "King of Man and Beasts" – this benevolent leader, teacher and grim avenger, who held sway from Grand Manan Island to the wintry shores of Labrador – was saddened to see Indian tribes still warring with one another and animals fighting among themselves.

So he departed, saying he would not return until conflict had left the earth. Old Indian story-tellers say he is still youthful, alive, and well at "the south end of the world," awaiting the glad day of his second home-coming.

How will the Indians know when he comes? Will they see him? Possibly not, because one Micmac tale says Glooscap was not visible to his people; they could only sense his presence. When he was angry, thunderous storms ravaged the countryside; when he was happy, Nature smiled.

Some scholars studying the history of the pagan early Indians say their conception of Glooscap was very close to the Christian belief.

It makes you think.

David and Goliath
Take to the Air

Out of the little down-east Maritime Provinces came two young men destined to join the élite circle of Canada's most famous fighter pilots in the First World War.

Thousands of hell-bent-for-leather combat fliers from the sparsely settled Dominion (population then seven million) swelled the ranks of the fledgling Royal Flying Corps. Amazingly, by 1918 Canadians constituted a third of the Royal Air Force officer enrolment. For the entire war, they represented also a quarter of the fatalities in Britain's air services.

This was the final chapter of spectacular single-handed combat in world history, the lineal descendant of the age of chivalry when armour-laden knights on horseback charged each other with lances at the level. It was an era of flying-helmets and goggles and open cockpits, of squadron leaders' long scarves fluttering back in the slip-stream, of Lewis machine guns mounted on the top wing to fire over the propeller, and of planes without parachutes – an age when sometimes a pilot, his bullet-riddled aircraft twisting downward in a trail of black smoke, waved a gallant salute to the victor. A romantic age perhaps, but also one of grisly tragedy.

Major Albert DesBrisay Carter, D.S.O. and Bar, Croix de Guerre, from Pointe de Bute in New Brunswick, didn't get to France until the end of 1917. He served only four and a half months before he was shot down, badly wounded, to be an unreported prisoner of war until the end of the conflict.

But in those few short months he became one of Canada's ranking fighter airmen: he gunned down an extraordinary total of thirty-one enemy planes. This number may not have compared with such renowned Canadian aces as Billy Bishop (seventy-two planes) and Collishaw (sixty), nevertheless it was higher than Eddie Rickenbacker's U.S. record of twenty-five kills.

And Carter not only distinguished himself as a patrol leader of "great keenness and dash," as one of his medal citations put it, but repeatedly ranged far behind the German lines in his versatile Sopwith Dolphin, strafing ground troops at such low level that they ducked in panic.

He survived many close brushes with death but, ironically, it was a German plane that killed Major Carter – after the war.

When the defeated enemy turned over its remaining aircraft to the Allies, the Canadian flier picked out a Fokker Flying Scout for his own use. He preferred it to British and French warplanes.

One day in 1919 he took up the Fokker for the entertainment of friends watching from the ground. Apparently he tried to put it through a sudden twist of a type the Fokker's strong structure couldn't withstand. Before the spectators' horror-stricken eyes the plane suddenly disintegrated, hurtling the great war flier to his death.

It's a shame that the exploits of these brave and selfless Canadians are so rapidly fading into the mists of time. What follows is another that should be preserved.

Captain Wendell Rogers developed a theory that became a burning obsession.

It was December 1917. A new and ominous menace had roared out of the daytime skies over the Ypres salient: massed flights of giant Gotha bombers, each squadron an armada bristling with machine guns, dropping high explosives on the British troops.

Word went around the Royal Flying Corps that it was sheer suicide to try to attack them. The superbombers – with a wingspread of nearly eighty feet and a body length of forty feet – could fire ahead, to the rear, and below through an opening in the fuselage. Together in close formation they were invincible.

They were undermining morale among the Allied soldiers in Flanders. Worse, squadrons of Gothas had emerged from the clouds over London, and intelligence reports said their eventual purpose was to launch a massive aerial assault on the British capital.

Wendell Rogers, a tall, erect and unassuming twenty-one-year-old from Alberton, P.E.I., refused to believe any plane was invulnerable.

Grandson of a former lieutenant-governor of Prince Edward Island, the Honourable Benjamin Rogers, he had studied at the University of Toronto, attended the Royal School of Artillery at Kingston, Ontario, before going to England to join the R.F.C. He was posted to No. 1 Scout Squadron in Flanders the spring of 1917.

Before being pitchforked into the front lines, Rogers had received only twenty-five hours of dual and solo flying time.

"I'd never seen the plane I was to fly," he commented matter-of-factly later. "They gave me three-quarters of an hour to become familiar with it."

But his flying skill soon won respect. By the time the youth first broached his Gotha theory in the officers' mess, he had shot down seven German aircraft. In one memorable exploit he proved that even with his Nieuport badly shot up he could regain the initiative, dive down and roar up under the belly of an enemy and blow the two-seater apart.

Nevertheless his idea was greeted with skepticism.

"There has to be one blind spot in the Gotha," insisted Rogers. "It's directly behind, where a Nieuport close in would be below the fire over the tail of the bomber and above the fire from below the fuselage."

He took his theory to the squadron commanding officer, who had cautioned his pilots against tackling needless hazards in trying to shoot down Gothas.

The dilemma of the C.O. can be imagined. Before him stood

a determined young officer supremely confident of his ability. But only the other day two Nieuports had been blasted out of the sky in a futile attempt to attack one of the juggernaut formations.

The C.O. tried to dissuade him, but cryptically added with a shrug and a sigh, "I hope you get the opportunity to prove you're right."

Just two days later the opportunity materialized.

On a chill gloomily overcast afternoon, Captain Rogers led four Nieuport Scouts on a patrol. Two went astray in the dense clouds. Hardly had the remaining three broken through the murk overhead than they espied seventeen black dots approaching in the sunshine at 10,000 feet – a flight of Gothas.

Then began a deadly game of manoeuvre. The Nieuports were swept by enemy fire as they passed underneath and zoomed upward. Then, from a high vantage point, the British fighters dived at the back of the formation. The three Gothas bringing up the rear accelerated to tighten ranks, but one was slower than the other two.

In a flash Rogers pounced on the laggard, plunging below its tail and then darting up to close in at a distance of only ten yards. Almost instinctively he pressed the trigger, pouring sixty bullets into the fuselage.

The Canadian stuck there like a leech, while enemy tracer bullets screamed over the wings and under the body of his tiny craft – for one false move would finish him.

Abruptly the huge Gotha swung left and headed downward, spurting crimson flames and emitting clouds of black smoke.

After fitting his Lewis gun with a new drum of ammunition, Rogers shadowed the diving giant to make sure it wouldn't last long enough to get behind the German trenches near Armentieres. Just as he was about to open fire again, two of the crew leaped out into mid-air, and almost immediately a tremendous blast blew the bomber apart. The fragments fell between the lines.

As one officer afterwards summed up the battle, "It was like a sparrow attacking a crow. The Nieuport's wingspread is less than a third of the Gotha's."

It was a day to remember back at the base when Rogers touched down. Not only had his victory made history, but it was to give a great psychological lift to the Allied fliers and ground forces on the Flanders front.

This heady feeling was reinforced when General Trenchard, chief of the Royal Flying Corps, sent a telegram to the squadron C.O.: "Congratulate the pilot who shot down the Gotha in flames . . . splendid work. . . . Let me know his name."

Although I met Wendell Rogers several times in Saint John in the 1920's, after he had lived in Charlottetown, and in Orillia and Oshawa, Ontario, it was a while before I even found out he had served in the Royal Flying Corps. Because of his reserved nature, he saw no reason to mention it.

It was only from other members of the Byng Boys' Club, whose bungalow occupies a commanding site overlooking the St. John River just above the famed Reversing Falls, I heard the story of "Monty" Rogers and the Gotha.

Still a young man after the war, as tall and slim and straight as ever, with aquiline features and a trim black mustache, he was taut and tense by nature, and modest to a fault.

For some reason I supposed his acute sensitivity, his keyed-up personality, were a result of nerve-wracking war service.

His friends said it was just the other way around: that instant responsiveness, that split-second reaction time, was what made him an outstanding pilot who destroyed ten enemy aircraft and won the Military Cross.

But to Monty Rogers there was only one pilot in that war. "Raymond Collishaw was the best I ever saw," he said. "Why, he could be almost on the ground and then loop his plane and touch down for a perfect landing."

As for aerial marksmanship, "There was no man who could shoot like Billy Bishop. He used to tell us, 'Just make sure nobody's going to get on my back, and I'll shoot them down for you.' And he did. He attacked big formations time and again, and got several of them."

Monty Rogers rarely referred to the fact that he had tangled repeatedly – all in a space of minutes – with the legendary Baron Manfred von Richthofen of Germany's Flying Circus. It was an eerie fight, a deadly game of "chicken" in the skies, in which they flew at each other head-on, each swerving aside in the last second.

Dr. Jack Edgecombe, still a practising dentist in his eighties, one of the four surviving First World War members of the club named after Baron Byng of Vimy in 1921, recalls hearing the story at first hand. "If one flier broke off too soon, the other would be on his back. If neither gave way, a smash-up was inevitable. Monty used to say, 'I'm thankful the good Lord always told me which way he was going to turn.' "

The strange encounter broke off when both duellists, running out of fuel, headed for their bases.

Wendell Rogers made Saint John his postwar home. He was one of the pioneers in organizing a flying club and a regional airline here and establishing an airport in his adopted city. He became president of SMT (Eastern) Ltd., the New Brunswick bus system, and president of the Dominion Motor Coach Association.

At the outbreak of the Second World War he was squadron leader in command of No. 117 (Fighter) Squadron, RCAF (Non-Permanent) at Saint John.

By a quirk of fate his industrial responsibilities in 1941 were widened to include the management of Canada Veneers, a plant turning out plywood to make the little ubiquitous deHavilland Mosquito bombers that proved to be such a scourge to the enemy on the Continent.

In 1949, with his two sons, Rogers established a plastics manufacturing firm. He died in 1967. His wife still resides in Saint John.

All four First World War members of the Byng Boys' Club were at a recent annual meeting – Dr. Edgecombe, Frank Wilson, Clarence Crocker, and Harry Heans – along with Second World War and Korean War veterans. And among past members they talked about was Monty Rogers – he of the nickname that sounded like the Second World War but really was an abbreviation for Montague, P.E.I. where his wife grew up – a long distance from Alberton, his own birthplace, by P.E.I. standards.

For that matter it would be difficult for anyone entering the Byng Boys' Club not to be reminded of Rogers. Its walls are decorated with scores of war mementos and photos – a spectacular collection – but overlooking the entire scene, in its new Union Club headquarters, is a black cross of the type that identified German warplanes. What strikes you immediately is its huge size.

A few days after Rogers had downed the Gotha, an Australian Colonel called at the squadron base, stayed for dinner and told the fliers about the epic air battle he had witnessed from the trenches.

"Some of my men crept out after dark to pick up souvenirs from the wreckage of the Gotha," he said. "Among other things they retrieved two big black crosses from a wing. I'd like very much to give one of them to that British pilot if I could only find him."

The Australian was startled when an officer informed him that the pilot, who was acting C.O. and host that day, was sitting right beside him.

The Uninvited Bedfellow

This is a story of an unusual human problem, told here with the thought in mind that others afflicted with the same terrifying symptoms as Mrs. Leaford – symptoms rare but far from unique – will realize there is very real hope. The names of the persons and places involved have been changed, but the events are from Mrs. Leaford's own narrative taped by the author, who also saw the parapsychologist's letters to her.

The first time she became aware that a peculiar entity was lurking around her, Mrs. Leaford said, was when she was visiting the home of a married daughter in the northern United States.

"On the night I arrived, I woke up with the feel of a man's body cuddled up close to me, behind me, with his arm around my waist, and he was giggling. He seemed to be quite mischievous."

This was the start of a nightmare that lasted seven years. In the quiet living room of her Moncton home the other day, Emily Leaford unfolded a frightening and almost incredible tale of what it is like to be "possessed" and yet unable to do anything about it.

Another married daughter, Beatrice, of Edmundston, N.B., was present and confirmed everything her mother said about family details and dates. Indeed, Beatrice had felt the chilling Presence herself – not in so personal a way, perhaps, but nevertheless enough to leave her fearful to the verge of panic when she had to walk past places where the unseen Thing hovered.

That first night, Mrs. Leaford continued, "I jumped out of bed. I was petrified. My husband was asleep in an adjoining room, the den. I woke him up and asked if he'd mind changing beds with me, because I couldn't sleep in that bed. He agreed; but the Presence followed me into the den. I said, 'Please don't scare me.'

"All of a sudden it pushed my arm away from the end of the pull-out bed – my arm just went flying – and it got right into bed with me. I couldn't get rid of it for quite some time. Finally it went away. Next morning I told my daughters, and they said, 'Well, don't tell anybody about it. They'll think you're crazy.' "

Interjected Beatrice: "But even before all this happened, I felt strange every time I went in that room."

Her mother added, "And whenever you went in the hall of that house – around the closet especially."

Beatrice: "And around the head of the stairs."

Mrs. Leaford continued, "This entity seemed to attach itself to me. It followed me home to New Brunswick. It would be in my bedroom often – I could feel a cold wisp of air across my face. But each time I went back to the States it seemed to be more prominent there, so I wasn't sure if it was the same one or I had one in each place."

We asked the daughter: Did the Presence make amorous or playful advances to her, too, or did she just feel it as a cold draught, or a cold breath?

"Not as a cold breath on me," she replied, and with a sigh of relief. "And no cuddling. My God, I would have died right there! No, when I visited my sister's in the States, and I walked into the living room or the front entryway, I felt a chill come over my body. It was just like I had hairs on my shoulders, they were all standing up, vibrating. I couldn't bear it. I haven't felt it lately; but I'm still leery of walking past those rooms. It's the first and only time I've ever been really afraid of anything."

Did Mrs. Leaford ever see the Presence materialize?

"In the fall of 1973 I went back to my daughter's in the U.S.," she answered, "and one night when I was sleeping in the sunporch I woke up and felt very strange – and I saw a tall form standing in the hall, outside the sunporch door. There was an orange aura around its feet, sort of a glow. At first I thought it was my daughter – she's tall – and then I said, 'Oh no, *no*. Not you again.'

"I was terrified, and I tried to get the light on – the light switch is just outside the sunporch door – but the switch wouldn't work; it wouldn't move. Then the Presence disappeared – the form disappeared – and the light came on.

"I practically ran to the other end of the house, and my daughter came in and talked with me. It followed me into the back of the house; it didn't do that originally, but it was getting bolder and bolder, as I said. It even began coming with me in my car at home, and later accompanied me to work. Before that it had generally visited me in my bedroom on a Sunday night, though I never could figure out why it chose Sunday."

Beatrice: "Mama, remember when it first started bothering you, you tried to get through to it and ask who it was and how it died?"

Mrs. Leaford: "Yes."

Beatrice: "And you sort of got the message that it had fallen down those stairs and broken its neck. You had visions of ambulances coming."

Mrs. Leaford: "I also got the message at that time that it was very tall, with red hair; that was about seven years ago. Then later when I actually saw the entity down there, the form *was* very tall – about six feet – but of course I saw no facial features. You got the message through feelings, rather than hearing or seeing."

One of the most fantastic happenings occurred at Christmas, 1973 – and it didn't befall only Mrs. Leaford this time but more particularly her New Brunswick daughter, Beatrice.

They were spending the holiday season at the mother's home, and early on Christmas Eve a son of Mrs. Leaford brought presents for everybody. The packages were placed under the gaily decorated fir tree.

A little while later Beatrice, sorting out the gifts and arranging them, exclaimed in surprise: "Did somebody move my present? I can't find it. I know he brought me one – it was right here – but it's gone!"

The family searched everywhere without avail. Somehow, inexplicably, a gift-wrapped box about twelve inches long had completely vanished.

Eventually they went to bed to await Santa's coming – but somebody else came to Mrs. Leaford.

She had never imagined she'd be annoyed tonight, because she was sleeping with her daughter's little son; but in the middle of the night she discovered there was a third party in the bed – and very definitely it was a case of three's a crowd.

For once she was more angry than scared, as she was very tired.

"Oh, will you go away and bother someone else tonight," she said in exasperation. "Go bother Beatrice or somebody; just leave me alone tonight!"

At this point in her story Beatrice took up the narrative:

"I awoke at two A.M. – that is, two o'clock on Christmas morning. Right away I knew there was something hanging around; I could feel it; I was getting all icy. I had no idea my mother had been bothered. I felt real cold – felt a very slight breeze, but a cold breeze. I sat right up and looked around.

"I had been sleeping on a couch in the living room by the Christmas tree, and I had a good view of the hall and stairway. *And there, floating through the air – elevated about four feet up – was my lost Christmas present.*

"Down the hall it floated – the box in green paper trimmed with red – around the corner and halfway up the stairs!

"The whole family had looked for it, and nobody could find it, and there it was, sailing up the stairs! I just couldn't believe it."

Was she sure she wasn't dreaming?

"There was no doubt I was wide awake. I could swear on a stack of Bibles I saw that present doing exactly what I described."

What happened then? Did the package remain halfway up the stairs?

"I finally got back to sleep. I was exhausted by all the preparations for Christmas. In the morning, my gift was right there under the Christmas tree where it had been in the first place.

"My mother figured that perhaps after she got cross at the Presence, it might have been bringing her my gift to make peace with her."

But if the Presence felt rebuked, its contrition didn't last very long. By the New Year it was pestering Mrs. Leaford so aggressively she could hardly keep on working at her job. The more she tried to fight it, the worse it became. She had violent headaches, she felt what seemed to be electric shocks going through her, she didn't want to go out anywhere, she was taking tranquillizers and other pills but was sitting up most of the night with cold cloths on her forehead because she couldn't lay her head down, even on three pillows.

Beatrice by now had become so revolted by the details of the entity's behaviour that she couldn't hear about it any more. "There were too many sickening aspects. I thought, my God, it can't be real, it just can't be real, it's too horrible."

In January 1974, Mrs. Leaford went to the United States to visit her other daughter and later to consult a famous parapsychologist, university professor, and lecturer with whom she had corresponded. Mrs. Leaford described the events following her arrival at the daughter's home:

"My daughter, who had turned Catholic with her husband, sprinkled holy water around one night. She burned candles. And she had *more* crucifixes on me – me, a non-Catholic! – at the end of it I was sleeping with a crucifix in my hand and one around my neck and one up on the bureau. And it seemed to be sort of afraid of this. It didn't bother me as much when I had these things around me.

"But my headaches had got so bad I went to see a doctor in her city, and he discovered I also had an extra heartbeat that I had picked up. I associated this with the entity."

The daughter accompanied her to a large city to see the parapsychologist. He proved to be a sympathetic and understanding man, who described Mrs. Leaford's symptoms as uncommon but very similar to others in his experience. He had also encountered the extra-heartbeat phenomenon previously. He didn't treat her case lightly at all, she said. Nor did he charge her for the consultation.

"He hypnotized me, and asked me to summon the entity there," said Mrs. Leaford. "He told me to ask it things, which I did. He told me to ask it if it wanted to leave and find a body of its own; and I got the message back that, yes, it did. I was hypnotized at the time, but I can remember some of the things that happened.

"He performed a rite of exorcism – not a church ceremony, of course, but his own procedure as a parapsychologist. He told the entity, by the powers invested in him, to leave or be cast into eternal darkness. But he talked to it very nicely.

"And it did leave me. When he woke me up, he said, 'How do you feel?' I said, 'I feel just wonderful.' I could even touch my head, and I shook my head, and said, 'Did we get rid of it?' and he said, 'Yes, it's gone; I felt it go.'

"I never had any heart trouble previously, and my heart is fine now. He told me I would have to be very careful – I was the kind of person who attracted these entities; the sex drive and psychic drive were very much the same thing, and I should have a full sexual life to avoid attracting them. He said I had been 'possessed,' which I didn't know; I just thought I was carrying my own ghost around. I knew I was nearly out of my mind; I looked terrible. If I hadn't written to him, and he hadn't seen me, I don't know where I would be now."

Since then Mrs. Leaford has found no trace of the entity at her U.S. daughter's home – nothing at all but some very vivid memories.

So is the malevolent spirit, in her opinion, gone for good?

"A month ago," she replied, "I felt I was attracting another one. I felt a presence in my bedroom. I was quite upset about it; I thought, 'Oh no, not again, I can't go through that again.' So I wrote to the parapsychologist and asked, 'Is it imagination or what?'

"He replied, no, I would always attract these entities; and he said, here is what you do. You picture a closed door, and the door is closed to this entity, and you talk to it very nicely and tell it that it must go away. Don't get cross, and don't force. He also said a salt bath helps break the spell."

Reassured, Emily Leaford says after seven years she feels today "like a new person." She can even look back and smile at some of the lighter aspects of her experiences.

Her daughter Beatrice is doubly glad.

She's glad her mother has made a wonderful comeback.

And she's particularly glad "the entity apparently didn't like me. It didn't go for me. Thank God for that."

Are Sea Monsters for Real?

"A creature with a head as big as a water pail and great green eyes raced around my canoe." – A summer resident of Grand Lake, N.B.

"The chief Medicine Man of the Micmacs swears that a fearful creature with head as big as a puncheon followed him and a brother Indian in their canoe some distance after the ice was cut this spring, snapping its bloody jaws in a most horrible manner." – E.J. Russell writing from Lake Utopia, N.B., 1872, in *Canadian Illustrated News*.

"Two women with their children went to the shore to do their week's washing. They took their washtubs and lunches and built a fire near the little wharf where the steamer docked just south of Scotsville. . . . Suddenly a child cried out in fright – all saw the great beast swimming toward shore. It had a long, hard body and a head like a cow, only bigger. They fled. The men had to go down to fetch the laundry and tubs after haying." – One of many monster stories related at Lake Ainslie in Cape Breton, N.S.

"It rose up five feet out of the water. My wife Lucie will tell you, too! Her hair was standing up like nails – her head hurt. The thing had humps like three upside-down boats, and eighty-five to ninety feet long. The tail splashed water thirty-five feet up in the air – not pails, tons of it. . . . A tail like a 747 jet!" – Louis Fournier describing one of numerous sightings in six-mile-long Lake Pohenegamook, Quebec, near the New Brunswick boundary.

It all began away back in prehistoric times, when Indians warned their children to watch out for ferocious denizens lurking in eastern Canada's rivers, lakes, and coastal waters.

"Ug-Wug" was a giant sea serpent in Micmac lore. He would leave his lair in the northern wilderness and swim southward, then turn around and swim up again, driving the first spring run of shad before him.

His summer home was in the Reversing Falls at Saint John, where he liked to romp and cavort in the biggest of the swirling whirlpools.

When the first recorded European explorers came, braves were often seen shooting arrows into logs gyrating wildly in the whirlpools – arrows with small packets of tobacco tied on as gifts to placate the evil spirit in the maelstrom

Accompanying Champlain at Port Royal in old Acadia in 1605, the French chronicler Lescarbot wrote that "Gou-Gou" the dragon lived in the Algonquin country – just about where Lake Pohenegamook is situated in Quebec about twenty-five miles west of the New Brunswick border.

Were Ug-Wug and Gou-Gou and their ilk just folktale characters, primitive bogey-men invented to keep misbehaving youngsters in line?

Not necessarily.

You'll find many a marine biologist in New Brunswick, Nova Scotia, Prince Edward Island, and Newfoundland who may readily deprecate the idea, for instance, that ghosts actually exist – but sea serpents are something else.

They want to keep open minds.

There have been too many very similar sightings, vouched for by responsible observers, not only at Loch Ness in Scotland and Ogopogo's Lake Okanagan in British Columbia, but also at Lake Pohenegamook in Quebec, Lake Ainslie in Cape Breton, in the harbours of Halifax and Liverpool on the Nova

Scotia mainland, off the seaward shore of Prince Edward Island, in lakes and coastal bays of Newfoundland – and in several lakes in New Brunswick.

"We must find a valid physical explanation for the very convincing reports that have come from places like Lake Ainslie and Lake Utopia," says Dr. Carl Medcof, a retired research scientist formerly with the St. Andrews, New Brunswick, Fisheries Biological Station. "Such reports should not be lightly dismissed. If we laugh at the people who report the sightings, we are the fools, not they."

Personally, he thinks some of the "monsters" could be balled-up eels – hundreds of them in one conglomeration, like worms dumped out of an angler's tin can. He has seen big clumps of eels such as those reported from time to time in Cape Breton's Lake Ainslie. These great free-floating spheres, espied in deep water just before the late-summer down-river migration, were described as "bobbing up and down slowly. . . . Sometimes actually breaking the surface."

One eel-ball was reportedly six feet in diameter, "big enough to fill two barrels," and "the flipping tails on the outside of the ball apparently caused a slow rolling."

Dr. Vadim Vladykov, professor emeritus of biology at the University of Ottawa, who once investigated the Lake Pohenegamook phenomenon for the Quebec government, is another scientist who refuses to discredit "monster" sightings as products of runaway imaginations.

"Something big has lived in the lake," he's convinced – and he's almost convinced it was a sturgeon. He learned that someone years ago released into the lake a young sturgeon, which may have grown to giant size.

"Eyewitnesses spoke of it having two sets of 'propellers,' in front and in the middle, which could have been the pectoral and ventral fins."

Science-fiction buffs attracted to this lake like to speculate that "Ponik," as the creature has come to be known, may be a marine reptile of a hundred million years ago, regenerated from a fertilized egg frozen since the glacial age.

Professional scientists aren't going to call them fools, either.

Professor Frederick Aldrich, director of biology at New-foundland's Memorial University, said it's not beyond the limits of possibility that some prehistoric animals, marooned by evolving land formations, have somehow managed to reproduce and evade extinction in a new environment.

He would find ready agreement among the many people who aver they saw the mysterious resident of broad seven-mile-long Lake Utopia near the Bay of Fundy coast. For some reason this monster is supposed to become re-activated around the time of the winter ice break-up – a sort of exuberant spring fever – threshing about vigorously as the water roils and froths, spewing logs and edgings up into the air.

The creature – which some say is forty feet long with a head like a horse – was reported first by lumberjacks in 1867, and intermittently since. So persistent were the early sightings by sawmill workers in Canada's Confederation year that local men set forth to catch it by attaching chains to logs near the shore – chains baited at the other end with salt fish and pork on huge hooks. They didn't get a nibble.

No more fortunate was a company organized at nearby St. George with a capital of $200 to trap the monster with 100-by-20-foot nets and other devices.

One of the most recent and thought-provoking sightings occurred in 1951. A grandmother in her mid-eighties, Mrs. Fred McKillop, Sr., of St. George, was sitting outside a summer cabin with two of her grandchildren just looking over the peaceful lake – and then:

"The water began to boil and made waves on the shore. A huge head broke out of the surface, then part of its body – it looked like a great black rock, but it was moving and splashing. I was so terrified I rushed the children into the cabin and locked the door. Later I realized we were in no danger – this was only a water beast – so we went outside and watched it going up and down the lake for quite a while."

She felt relieved at suppertime when the men came home from a fishing trip and told her the story of the Lake Utopia sea serpent, for she feared she was seeing things. And she felt better, again, when two groups of anglers on the lake reported they, too, saw inexplicable roiling of the waters and a strange unidentified creature.

Less well known, even in New Brunswick, is the fact that many residents around the shores of Grand Lake say they've seen a monster in this, the biggest lake in the province, a part of the 450-mile-long St. John River system.

Descriptions of the Thing have ranged as big as thirty feet long and four feet in breadth. One man asserted "a creature with a head as big as a water pail and great green eyes raced around my canoe, not on just one occasion but year after year." Others say they saw the deep wet furrow in the sand and gravel where the hulk had slithered along the shore. (James Woodbury reported finding the same kind of slimey trail, eighteen inches wide, from Lake Utopia to the nearby Bay of Fundy.)

Grand Lake folk don't panic easily; they look for a logical explanation. Some think their mystery resident may be a giant eight-foot eel; others say a huge turtle (they've been captured here up to fifty-five pounds); others say a seadog; but the favourite version is that the monster is a huge sturgeon. These long-snouted, armour-plated fish, once common in the St. John River, grow to twelve or even fifteen feet and a weight of 200 pounds. They frighten the daylights out of underwater swimmers because they look as fierce as sharks. But sturgeons are as docile as cows. In the old days fishermen went out in their flat-bottomed "sturgeon boats," netted them, roped them by their squarish tails, and tethered them to posts until it was time to ship them to the Boston market.

Another theory: The Grand Lake monster could be a family of otters: "They sometimes loop in line together going through the water."

But the superstitious will remind you that otters don't have a head as big as a water pail, nor eels a head like a horse.

Still another: A.C. Holman at New River Beach, not far from Lake Utopia, wrote to Dr. Medcof that a pulpwood cutter driving his truck near the Mount Pleasant nickel mine saw something strange in the early-morning half-light at MacDougall Lake. He thought someone had dumped a load of gravel on the road.

"He stopped his truck, and then saw the thing was moving across the highway towards a small lake – a giant turtle at least four feet long. I am convinced there are some very large turtles around here."

Which brings to mind that many of the sightings in the Atlantic provinces have mentioned "turtle-like humps" on the monster.

In support of his theory, Mr. Holman later wrote that he talked with E.J. Clark, a woods official with a pulp company, who takes the prevalence of big turtles "more or less as a matter of course, and even has some photos of them. . . . One close-up snap was enough to scare anyone to death with large and appalling claws, and a jack-o-lantern face."

Added Mr. Holman, "There are stories about a sea serpent in Loch Lomond about ten miles east of Saint John, too."

Loch Lomond is a broad and deep lake, set in rolling countryside, which reminds Scots of its storied namesake in the Old Country. Down through the years it has been known for its occasional mammoth-sized brown trout. Does something bigger, and more terrifying, also live in the depths of Saint John's great water-supply reservoir? (But Saint John is famous for the pristine superb quality of its water, and there is no record of anyone finding a sea serpent in a glassful unless he mixed something with the water first.)

Matter of fact, there may be mysteries hidden in numerous other expanses of water in the Atlantic provinces.

"Did you ever notice," Dr. Medcof muses, "how many of our lakes are called 'Serpent Lake'? And most of them aren't serpent-shaped at all."

The Most Poignant Character

It would be hard for anyone to name offhand what episode in New Brunswick's history – real or folklore – touches his inner feelings most deeply.

If I were asked quickly, I'd probably say Lady LaTour's valiant last defence of her husband's fort at the mouth of the St. John River against Sieur d'Aulnay Charnisay, climaxed by her being forced to watch the hanging of her garrison, one by one, with a rope around her own svelte neck.

Then I'd remember John Gyles, the little nine-year-old Maine boy, captured in 1689 by the Maliseet Indians who had massacred his father – a stripling who served for seven and a half years as a slave of the Indians and later a French family on the St. John River.

But then the Maliseet heroine Malabeam would come to mind – and Malabeam would probably win out because she willingly sacrificed her life, or her sanity, to save her people.

Historians disagree as to whether bloody family conflicts ever erupted among the Maliseets, Micmacs, Passamaquod-dies, and Penobscots, all Abenaki tribes (although the neigh-bouring Micmacs and Maliseets spoke such different dialects they couldn't understand each other).

In the shadowy mists of history are reports that long ago these two tribes met in terrible battles.

Both, along with their New England cousins, were fierce and merciless in pre-dawn assaults on English colonial towns as allies of the French.

But little of a gory nature took place within the borders of New Brunswick, except for recurrent forays by the Mohawks down from the north woods. Until modern times, New Brunswick Indians kept their children well-mannered by threatening to call the cannibalistic Mohawks, the "human wolves," the most blood-thirsty of all the Iroquois.

That's why the Maliseets built the wooden pallisaded fort at Meductic that John Gyles knew – not because of peril from the revenging New Englanders, but to protect them from Mohawk war parties ranging down the St. John River from the St. Lawrence in Quebec.

And that's doubtless why around the campfires the Maliseet and Micmac sachems loved to spin tales of great victories over the dreaded Mohawks, victories often won by clever strategy rather than weight of numbers.

Like the time that the Micmacs built a large campsite on the shore of the Woolastook (St. John) stream, and the braves formed a hunting party and went into the leafless November forest for moose and caribou.

Suddenly loud raucous war whoops and feminine screams – "the Mohawks!" – rent the peaceful early morning air.

The fired-up attackers were disappointed to catch no warriors off guard. Then they set a trap. Rather than slaughter the women, they took away one as a prisoner – Nemissa, the comely wife of the absent chief – knowing that the others would urge the returning Micmacs to pursue and rescue her.

No avenging flotilla came that night, however – only a shadowy lone canoe bearing Nemissa's husband and a friend, Black Feather. They espied the Mohawks' smouldering campfire, beached their canoe, and crept toward the big wigwam where the sated war party was sleeping after a feast.

Nemissa, mending Mohawk moccasins near the flap of the wigwam, immediately recognized her husband's belt when he silently pushed it along the ground into her sight, and she tiptoed out.

Moments later her husband had strung a trip-line of hide across the entrance. At a signal, all three doused the campfire with water from bark vessels, plunging the place into darkness. They started yelling a bedlam of Micmac war cries.

Wildly, the bleary Mohawks flailed about at each other within the wigwam, thinking the enemy was in their midst, and then as they tripped out over the entrance barrier they were felled by Micmac tomahawks.

Only four wounded Mohawks were spared.

"Begone!" the triumphant chief ordered. "Tell your brothers at home what kind of a welcome they can expect if they set foot in our domain again."

There are many legends of this pattern – the Micmacs and Maliseets winning against great odds. Sometimes the defenders were warned by prophetic vision – like a wide-eyed squaw bursting into an encampment crying, "There is trouble! I see a great party of Mohawks encamped behind that mountain, and when darkness descends they wish to slay us all!"

The outnumbered quarry (reminisced Old Gabe, an ancient Indian living in recent times above Fredericton) devised a ruse – a "great dance to make the Mohawks think we are all celebrating a feast," but the braves would gradually steal away, leaving only the old men and squaws to continue.

They agreed on Nature sounds, like bird calls, to communicate with one another in the darkness. Any Indian who could not reply in kind would be instantly killed and his head tossed in among the dancers.

So stealth met stealth as the Mohawks crawled through the thick brush – and many a head was thrown into the noisy dance, accompanied by the exhortation, "Dance faster!"

As dawn came up, the dancers were collapsing from weariness. But all the Mohawks except four were dead. The survivors, their ears and noses cut off, were freed to return home and show their tribe what trespassers could expect.

The warlike Mohawks, however, apparently were slow to take hints.

Another time their approach was detected by a perceptive Micmac squaw, Anakwa. With her cousin, Chichook, she had accompanied her husband on the first day of a hunting trip by canoe. Both women for some reason felt uneasy forebodings about the beach that Kakloogwak, the husband, chose to put up their birch-bark wigwam, an anxiety which amused him; he laughingly derided their premonitions.

But next day Anakwa saw something that froze her blood: large numbers of wood chips were floating down the river.

"Look!" she exclaimed to her cousin. "They are fresh and they are not cut by the beaver, but by Indian hatchets. Strangers are building a place to ford the stream and attack us!"

When her husband returned from his early-morning hunt, they paddled hastily toward their faraway village to sound the alarm.

But first (and at this juncture you have to strain your imagination a bit and remember we're recalling a legend), Kakloogwak fastened his magical bag of fox pelts to a tree.

"I will return for you," he confided to the pouch, "but meanwhile if any hostile Indians come in sight, bark twice."

They paddled on for some time, then went ashore to camp till morning – but in the middle of the night they heard two sharp barks in the distance.

Rushing home, the three aroused the Micmac village, and immediately the chief gave orders to get a bounteous repast ready to welcome the visitors. It was only right, he reminded them, to entertain a foe before a battle.

The Mohawk braves, surprised in their turn, feasted heartily with them and sang war songs until dawn.

Then, when at last the Mohawk chief seized his hatchet and challenged the host to fight, the waiting Micmac braves sprang at the strangers and annihilated them within minutes.

On another occasion, it is related, a Maliseet brave spotted a Mohawk encampment through a thicket of cherry trees, near where the Muniac empties into the St. John River. He ran to his hidden canoe, paddled frantically for Aughpak, the head of the tide near the mouth of the Keswick, but discovered to his dismay that all but five of the warriors had gone to Passamaquoddy Bay to fish for pollock.

The six braves sought the counsel of the chiefs, and one of the wise old men broached a desperate plan.

"You say the Mohawk wigwams crowd the shore opposite the tip of the big peninsula," he said. "So portage from here across the peninsula, two braves to a canoe, and paddle around the point and then back down here. Keep out of range of their arrows. Do this until you no longer can paddle."

Thus began an exhausting ordeal, for after several round trips the light birchbark canoes became almost like stone weights on the warriors' heads and arms. The squaws at home constantly refreshed them with Indian soup and maize cakes.

Somehow (according to Old Gabe) the Maliseet warriors kept up the delusion for three days – and, as far as the apprehensive Mohawks knew, for three nights, too.

"Their braves are as many as the leaves on the trees!" exclaimed a Mohawk chief. "They must have known we were coming, and summoned all their allies."

It was remarkable then, as now, how sheer power can change aggressive intentions.

The Mohawks sent out an interpreter to mid-river to ask one of the Maliseets for a pow-wow. What the invaders really hoped for, he explained, was a lasting peace.

All six Maliseet braves, fearsome-looking with eagle-feather bonnets, and red earth rubbed into their faces, boldly paddled to the Mohawk camp next day. At home, they said, were a thousand warriors waiting and eager to go into battle.

A wrinkled old Mohawk sachem assured them, "I seek only quiet and friendship. Let us bury the hatchet, and we will depart and I will be content to face my remaining days in peace."

With due ceremony a stone hatchet was buried in a hole dug in the river, filled in by stones anchored by a great rock.

And so, Old Gabe avers, the long strife ended forever. And the hatchet of peace still reposes somewhere below the ripples of the gentle river.

The most haunting legend of the Maliseets originated long before the first white explorers ventured up the St. John River.

Historians relate slightly different versions. Some call the heroine Malabeam, others Malobiannah.

Some say a Mohawk advance war party captured a Maliseet hunter and his family on the Madawaska River. They slaughtered the man and the children, but spared the squaw, Malabeam, on condition she would guide them down to the St. John River and the Maliseet Fort Meductic.

Others insist Malabeam was the lovely daughter of a hunter and his squaw, who were killed on the spot.

St. John River historian Dr. W.O. Raymond wrote that on reaching the Madawaska the Mohawks overwhelmed a Maliseet fort courageously defended by Grand Sachem Pemmyhaouet and 100 braves. The only survivor was Malabeam, the betrothed of Pemmyhaouet's slain son.

On what happened immediately after, however, everyone agrees:

Seething with hatred for her abductors, Malabeam tried not to show her tears. She sat quietly in a leading chief's canoe as the 500 Mohawk warriors paddled down the stream.

Dutifully she told them where to portage to avoid the Little Falls at the mouth of the Madawaska, and they soon entered the placid waters that lead several miles to Grand Falls.

When night fell, the canoes were lashed together to drift onward. Most of the Indians dozed while a few braves guided and steered the strange armada, taking directions from the tensely waiting Malabeam.

Gradually to the ears of the paddlers came what seemed to be a distant roar. It grew louder, awakening some of the Mohawks.

"What is that rumbling sound?" a chief demanded of Malabeam. "Is it a waterfall?"

"Yes, but at the mouth of a stream that empties into the Woolastook," the girl calmly assured them. "We will pass it in a few moments."

The chief settled back to watch expectantly.

And so they neared the brink of one of the great cataracts of eastern North America, known to the Maliseets as Chik-un-ik-pe, "the destroying giant."

Now the huge raft of canoes was moving at a quickening pace. In desperation the Mohawks seized their paddles and dug deep into the foaming waters, but nothing could break the death grip of the powerful current.

Here once again the legends diverge. Some say Malabeam slipped over the side of her canoe just in time to strike out for shore, the furious shouts of her captors lost in the thunder of Grand Falls ahead.

Most historians adhere to the version that she was swept over the precipice with the Mohawk horde, her victorious battle cry just a faint echo in Nature's deafening tumult.

Yet others contend she somehow lived through the terrifying experience of the seventy-five-foot plunge, managed to retrieve a lone unbroken canoe in the raging white gorge below, and paddled down to Fort Meductic. There, exhausted and hysterical, she wailed, "Mohawks! Mohawks!" and Maliseet braves rushed to the river to carry her inside the stronghold.

As her story was unfolded, and later confirmed by the corpses washed up ashore below Grand Falls, she became a heroine of the tribe forever – but a heroine who was left mentally deranged.

The Bombastic American – from Canada

Down the steep streets of San Francisco rumbled a trumpeting parade led by a ringmaster atop an elephant, doffing his pink top hat to the throng and tossing out certificates entitling the recipient to a circus ticket and a tooth pulled free afterwards.

Many bedazzled onlookers thought it must be the famous P.T. Barnum, master of sugar-coated bunkum and dean of American showmen.

But the laughing ringmaster, clad in a green satin suit, was none other than famous dentist Painless Parker. He had bought a marooned circus for $50,000, and was putting it to work advertising him up and down the Pacific coast.

Most surprisingly, he wasn't an American at all. He was a member of a northern race notorious for innate conservatism, stolidity, and shyness.

He was a Canadian.

No one could have possibly imagined all that circus whoop-de-do in 1872, when Edgar Randolph Parker was born of upright Bible-reading Baptist parents in the small Bay of Fundy village of Tynemouth Creek, N.B.

The only early clue, perhaps, was that Ned Parker – "Hokey," as he was known – had a fiercely independent streak. He attended public school, a Baptist seminary, Acadia University, and fared the same in all of them – he was repeatedly kicked out for obstreperous mischief.

His father got him a job in a Saint John hardware store –

but on the first day Ned discovered his pay was to be only $1.50 a week. That did it.

He ran away to sea, got into scrapes, returned and peddled wares from door to door, ran away again – and while in Barbados recuperating from an injury was impressed by the importance the hospital staff attached to the white-coated doctors. Ned told his parents he wanted to be a doctor. They could afford only $250, suggesting he become a dentist instead.

That was the turning-point of a dramatic life story.

Ned returned all duded up in city clothes from studies in New York and Philadelphia – still a youth of twenty – and opened a dental office in the St. Martins barber shop. No one came – practically no one, that is. He took in, gross, an average of twenty-five cents a month.

George Mallory, the local druggist, put his finger on the trouble. "Going to church, as you've been doing, Ned, won't help you in their eyes. People here are just scared of dentists; they're afraid you'll hurt them."

So in 1894 Ned Parker tried something different: Noisy, blatant showmanship. In the Hampton area, twenty-five miles distant, he harnessed his horse to a gaudily painted wagon, stopped occasionally, and blew mighty blasts on a dinner horn to draw people.

He gave a scholarly lecture on dental hygiene, then launched into a broadside designated to appeal to betting men's instincts: "For only twenty-five cents I will extract your tooth," he cried, "but if it causes you any pain, I will give you five dollars!"

He attracted crowds, of course; but did he lose a fortune? Not according to one aging gentleman I talked with years ago, Walter C. Brown of Saint John, then eighty-nine, who as a boy in 1894 watched the great medicine show at the old Saint John Exhibition.

After Dr. Parker's emotional spiel, he recalled, up to the platform shambled a rustic youth holding on to his aching jaw.

The dentist seated him in a leather reclining chair, felt his swollen face, looked into the mouth, surreptitiously picked up his forceps, nodded to the banjo player and drummer sitting

79

on either side of the patient – and immediately a wild banging cacophony of sound broke out.

Moving so rapidly the eye could hardly follow, Painless Parker within moments held high a tooth in his shining forceps; the onlookers were clapping and whistling shrilly.

The patient – or victim – sat there gawking, feeling his jaw.

"You didn't even feel it, did you?" Painless Parker was prompting in his ear. "It was all in your imagination!"

The bumpkin nodded numbly.

Said Walter C. Brown, "I'll never forget it. What a natty dresser he was, and how fast his hands worked. A country fellow beside me kept saying, 'By sweet lightning! How he does it!' "

Well, how *did* he do it? Observers differ. Unquestionably he had tremendous self-confidence, or he wouldn't have had the gall to distribute these handbills all over Saint John:

A Grand Open-Air Concert Twice Daily, with Vocal and Instrumental Music and Teeth Extracted Free of Charge Without Pain. . . . Nothing to Corrupt the Morals of the Most Refined or Fastidious Person in the City. The extractions would be effected by a Peculiar Method of His Own, With Whips, Swords, Spoons and Instruments of His Own Invention.

Opinions today mostly concur that Painless Parker possessed a lightning-fast forceps hand, a penetrating knowledge of human nature—and perhaps a grasp of legerdemain and hypnosis.

He *wasn't* painless at all, another oldster told me. Eighty-year-old Melvin W. Parke said: "As far as I ever found out, he just rubbed a little cocaine on the gum. Some country folks allowed he used only cold spring water."

Mr. Parke, as a boy at Big Salmon River, trekked to St. Martins one day to have an ulcerated back tooth taken out. "And it hurt like blazes for three weeks. It hurt even more than when a schooner captain pulled out a tooth for me with a pair of pliers!"

But showmanship, ability, intense desire, and unmitigated cheek can make up for small deficiencies. Painless Parker was on his way to becoming the biggest-earning dentist in the world. Like Barnum, he would use blimps, elephants, camels, high-wire walkers, jugglers, clowns, marching bands – but he also, on request, publicly pulled the aching teeth of tigers, lions, and walruses in the centre ring of the big top. He even implanted diamonds in the teeth of former heavyweight great Bob Fitzsimmons.

These were only the prelude. Even more mind-boggling stunts were to come. On the side of his New York building blossomed a sign: "I Am Positively 'It' in Painless Dentistry, Yes Sirree." Another sign, more than 100 feet tall, next proclaimed: "Painless Parker, Peculiarly Pleasing to Particular Patients and Philanthropically Disposed to Popular Prices."

As gaggles of people stared up, a man leaned out a window – Painless Parker himself, carmel-coloured beard and all – and hollered down: "Come one, come all, everybody! You won't feel anything!"

Then, startlingly, an aerialist walked a tight rope from the next high building to his building, shouting: "I'm going to Painless Parker's, he doesn't hurt a bit!" A minute or two later he reappeared, walking the other way: "I've been to Painless Parker's. He didn't hurt at all!"

Whenever the tight-rope artist rested, a human fly started clambering up the exterior of the building, yelling the same message, going and coming.

Above all, Painless Parker was a fighter. Under constant verbal and legal attack for years, he dodged, ducked, feinted, swerved – and usually came back with a devastating counter-punch.

The people who harassed him relentlessly were the "ethicals" – orthodox dentists – who were horrified by his razzle-dazzle self-promotion techniques.

It wasn't easy to corner him. When the profession got a law enacted to force dentists to use their own name in practice, Painless Parker promptly got a court order changing his first name from Edgar to Painless.

When they won out in an application to suspend his licence to practise, Dr. Parker retained his income by leasing to his employees the chain practice he had built up. By this time he had forty dental parlours from New England to California and Vancouver, B.C., and a staff of 1,000, including 250 dentists. His annual gross income was about $5,000,000.

(Some of his own dentists, aware of the professional shadow they lived under, left for home at the end of the day with their coat collars pulled up and hats pulled down. Their wavering loyalty didn't faze Painless Parker. He filled gaps in his staff with reformed alcoholics he salvaged in a special project of his own.)

He became adept at rapid-talking himself out of going to jail for lack of a local licence. Failing once early in his career, he slammed down his new "Dentist" sign over the head of a Pacific Coast law official and went to jail feeling much better.

But Painless Parker always bounced back, and soon he was driving east toward New Brunswick – with his dental technician, who doubled as banjoist and cornetist – just a few days after his advance agent, who was plastering little towns with extravagant posters about the wonder man.

He had married Frances Wolfe of Brooklyn, a nineteen-year-old piano student who once rapped on his door to protest the loud racket being made by a cornetist – namely Painless, trying to become expert enough to dispense with his own cornetist – and he brought her to New Brunswick for the honeymoon.

Naturally, to earn a few extra dollars to spend on his bride, Painless Parker pulled a few teeth. In no time he was in jail because his licence had expired. He paid the two-dollar licence, got out – and then engaged a troupe of minstrels to play an ear-splitting concert in a vacant lot that happened to be next to the dental registrar's home in Moncton.

And often he chuckled, as he looked over his magnificently equipped ranch in the Santa Clara valley of California, "I keep this place not only for the wife and the three children, but to make the ethicals green-eyed with envy."

Probably he had the same idea, earlier in his career, when

he owned a stable of beautiful horses, including a matched pair that took his bright red carriage up Riverside Drive every afternoon, with the principal passenger in his red silk dustcoat and red silk hat waving to admiring passers-by. Later he acquired a bevy of fine automobiles, including a gold-toned chauffeur-driven limousine. And, oh yes – an ocean-going yacht.

Painless Parker had the opportunist's knack of turning liabilities into assets. When hired hecklers tried to disrupt his Coney Island show, where twice daily he yanked teeth in public while wearing a white frock coat and beaver top hat, the dentist retorted indignantly:

"Young men, where are the high-fee dentists who are paying you to try to block my intention to give the working class a fair deal? I extract a tooth painlessly for only fifty cents, just four bits. What do your sponsors charge?"

The gathering muttered, and roared back: "Throw them out!"

There were two ironic things about Painless Parker. He really tried, time and again, to drop the "Painless" and practise as a regulation dentist, usually to please his wife, who shrank from his promotional extravaganzas. But each time he nearly starved. A compulsive empire-builder, he soon started organizing another chain.

And deep down, he felt hurt about being forever hounded by the ethicals. After all, as he repeatedly told close friends, he had accomplished great things for the profession. He introduced three chairs for each of his dentists, so they wouldn't have to stand by idle while fillings hardened. He paved the way for "group dentistry" – all specialties, including even financing and collections, under one roof. He took pride in making ordinary people conscious of the importance of dental hygiene and in removing their apprehensions about dentists. Not only that, but he was the first to bring soothing background music into dental emporiums, even though it was a faint echo of his early rambunctious musical accompaniments.

After the Second World War, a widower now, Painless Parker came back more often to boyhood scenes in New Brunswick. He was still an elegant dresser, but his taste in his subdued seventies now ran to banker's suits rather than cowboy hats and shiny high leather boots. With his white goatee he looked distinguished, like a Kentucky colonel; some compared him to Buffalo Bill Cody, while later onlookers remarked how much he looked as if he owned a fried-chicken chain.

He liked to visit his old friend, theatre magnate F.G. Spencer, in Saint John and study the picture of the Leinster Street School class on the office wall.

"Man, oh man," he would ejaculate, "just look at our teacher! What a whack Bella Nugent could give you if you acted the fool!"

Painless Parker died in 1952 at eighty. Despite his advanced years, he was still an active and happy man. Recently, belatedly, his licence had been restored – and so he was starting to extract teeth again.

Ghosts – and Where to Find Them

"Where can I see a good ghost?"

I've been asked this enthusiastic question a hundred times since I wrote a book called *Ghosts, Pirates and Treasure Trove*: *The Phantoms that Haunt New Brunswick*.

For some reason, no one wants to see a bad ghost. They always insist on a good one. Fortunately most New Brunswick ghosts are a pretty friendly lot.

Your chances are promising almost anywhere in this province. It has had four and a half centuries of so-called Western civilization – and perhaps as much as 106 centuries of habitation altogether – to build up an imposing folklore gallery of phantoms, witches, wizards, presences, poltergeists, and spirit gods, because archaeologists now say traces of humans living here go back 10,600 years.

There are ghosts that never utter a word, and ghosts that give vent to blood-chilling screams, like the Dungarvon Whooper of the Miramichi woods. There are ghosts that thump as they walk up the stairs, and silent ghosts that leave no footprints in the snow. There are ghosts of French explorers, English freebooters, king's governors, chuckling Indians, a bishop's wife, boat rowers, flaming ships, frustrated lovers, heroes and heroines, and especially headless people, including a headless nun.

A surprising number of New Brunswickers, apparently, have lost their heads over the years. This is the likeliest phenomenon you will encounter. I've talked with motorists all the way from broad Chaleur Bay in the north to verdant sea-girt Grand Manan in the south who swear they've driven right through a headless man who came running out in front of their car – but no corpse could be found afterward. A Fredericton doctor did it twice, to his horror, at the same place at the same early morning hour in two successive years.

Why these strange goings-on? Are they due to the sea mists on three sides of the province, and land fog in the inland hollows?

Sister Catherine Jolicoeur of Edmundston, who collects sightings of phantom ships all over the world, isn't sure. But she knows it happens.

"At Pokemouche, going toward Tracadie, just before you reach the church," she says, "there's a small woods on the right. Just a few months ago, in the spring, an apparition jumped out in front of a car and the driver swerved into the ditch. The driver was shaken. It had looked exactly like a man without a head.

"Two weeks later another motorist reported the same experience."

Evidently this unnerving spirit has been around a long time. Adds Sister Jolicoeur, "When I was teaching in Paquetville in November, 1974, my students said Leon Smith saw a headless man while driving through Pokemouche the night before.

"I paid no attention; I thought it was a joke. But several students and adults told me more details. They said the car went right over him, but Leon couldn't find a body. No one else was there."

This posed quite a quandary for Leon. He knew he should inform the police – but how can a driver tell the police, "I ran over a headless man but couldn't find him?"

Eventually he did notify them, Sister Jolicoeur continues, and to his surprise the Mountie asked, "Was the victim dressed in grey?"

Leon said eagerly, "Yes, he had a grey overcoat on. I saw him clearly in the headlights."

"Did the man have a head?"

Leon didn't like to admit it, at first. Then he mustered his resolve and confessed, "I didn't have much time to look – but I don't *think* he had a head."

The Mountie closed the report book and commented with a sigh, "That fits the description."

What about those phantom ships off the north, east, and south coasts of New Brunswick? Are they more likely to be seen than two-legged apparitions?

Probably. Over the years, hundreds of people along the Bay Chaleur shore have watched eerie rising and falling columns of light illuminating the sky as a phantom blazing ship glided rapidly past. They include observers of unimpeachable integrity – ministers, priests, nuns, Sunday school teachers, and their entire flocks. A rare few have seen the phenomenon twice.

But thousands of others on the coast have never noticed a glimmer, so naturally they tend to be skeptical.

One middle-aged man I talked with groused, "Nobody ever sees the fireship except idiots and drunks."

I reminded him his own brother claimed to have watched the phenomenon twice.

Repeated the man with emphasis, "I said nobody except idiots and drunks."

Scientists shrug off local superstitions about ghosts of ill-starred square-riggers and doomed pirate ships, and say the fireship is probably a phosphorescent or electrical manifestation before a storm, perhaps related to what old-time mariners called "St. Elmo's Fire."

"Science hasn't explained everything yet, even about phantom ships," Sister Jolicoeur comments. "I'm sure it's a natural phenomenon, but also psychological. It fills a need – satisfies a need – for the onlookers' sense of justice. The idea of a pirate ship burning up reaffirms the belief that the bad are punished and the good are rewarded. They connect it with hell."

Occasionally New Brunswick spectres take the form of animals – pigs, horses, and particularly dogs. Stories of big black baleful-eyed dogs – often the precursors of calamity – have held listeners spellbound in the Miramichi River country, on

Partridge Island at the mouth of Saint John harbour, and on the island of Grand Manan to the south. Inevitably they bring to mind ancient Welsh folk tales about "the hounds of hell."

Some ghosts, I've learned, are predicted by the calendar with unerring accuracy. For instance the Rowing Man is heard loudly working the oarlocks in his fishing dory somewhere off the shore of Little Dark Harbour, Grand Manan, in the tranquil moonlight during one week of the year only – between November 19 and 25. But he never materializes to human eyes.

And April 18 is the magic date for the Codfish Man. If you happen to be strolling around West Saint John that evening, fishermen say, you may see a man clad in oilskins and sou'wester trudging up from the wharves carrying a giant codfish over his shoulder – a cod so huge it hangs down his back and forces him to walk slightly bent forward, like the label picture of an old well-known brand of cod liver oil emulsion.

"You can almost catch up to him," recalls a believer, "but then he vanishes and reappears thirty feet past you. Later you may meet him walking back to the harbour – without the fish."

It is told that one day in the sailing era many years ago, the port fishing fleet put out into the Bay of Fundy in the hope of big catches. Hours later an unexpected gale whiplashed the bay. A few lucky men managed to row their boats back into the harbour, others ran theirs up on the rocks along the coast – but Daniel Keymore, who had forayed far out, wasn't among them.

Two days later his anchored boat was discovered upside down; but no sign of the fisherman.

For Mrs. Keymore and children at home, the next April 18 was a date that brought poignant memories – and a mystery: The morning after, they found a big fresh codfish on their verandah.

Eventually the widow remarried, taking up residence in a new house on the harbour front. And three days later, at midnight April 18, her old home suddenly erupted in a mass of flames and burned to the ground.

Next morning nothing remained to remind anyone of its past – except a great fresh codfish lying in front of the smoking ruins.

But the ghost – or presence – that continues to fascinate me most is the female phantom of Gagetown, a gracious old village overlooking the scenic St. John River.

She inhabits the 1810 estate of famous weaver and internationally known tartan designer Patricia Jenkins – a two-and-a-half-storey residence with four chimneys in a pastoral setting dominated by ancient linden, oak, pine, maple, ash, black locust, hawthorn, and boxwood trees.

This is the famous presence who, while apparently benign, mischievously removed an oil painting from the walls time after time and left it on the floor below. She was reportedly seen on several occasions by the late Very Reverend Dr. Charles T. Boyd of Petersville. Though normally invisible, the presence was often followed across the parlour by the wide-staring eyes of Miss Jenkins' cat, slowly swivelling its head. The presence was immediately "felt," if not seen, by at least four hypersensitive visitors at different times; they suggested, from the feelings in their shoulders, that an awful tragedy had once befallen the mansion.

Pat Jenkins later learned from a descendant of the original Scottish owner, the Honourable Hugh Johnson, that his eldest daughter married an Englishman and died in childbirth; and that one of the sons and his fiancée drowned in the spring river freshet when their carriage overturned.

My ghost book had hardly appeared in print when Mrs. Peggy di Carlo of Minto, in the Grand Lake area, told me an intriguing historical tale. She expressed surprise that Miss Jenkins evidently had not known of it.

Mrs. di Carlo had spent her childhood summers visiting her aunt, Mrs. Frank Mahony, in what was later to become the Jenkins home at Gagetown.

Perhaps fortunately for twelve-year-old Peggy Lucas, she had never heard of a ghost in the old mansion. She wasn't expecting to see anything out of the ordinary.

So the night it happened, when she was sleeping in an upstairs bedroom, she was more baffled than scared.

"All of a sudden," she recalls, "I awakened just as a lady in white walked slowly from the direction of the closet right past my bed, toward the window. Her hair was down around her shoulders. I saw her plainly.

"A strong wind was blowing the curtains back into the room at the time, and naturally I thought it was my aunt going to shut the window. She always wore her hair in a bun, and let it down at night.

"I said, 'What's wrong, Aunt Margaret?' – but there was no answer. Then, just as suddenly, the lady in white vanished before my eyes.

"I spent the rest of the night propped up on my pillow staring at the window, I was so puzzled."

What did her aunt say about it next day?

"Nothing. I didn't dare tell anybody. I was afraid I'd be scoffed at – they'd tell me, 'You silly little girl, you were just dreaming.'"

Mrs. di Carlo heard or saw nothing more of an unusual nature about the house for thirty years.

"Then the whole family gathered four or five years ago for Aunt Margaret's funeral in Saint John," she recollects. "Afterward my uncle, James Dalton of Chipman – Aunt Margaret's twin brother, by then in his nineties – began reminiscing."

He said that in the last century a Saint John young lady went up to Gagetown for a gala social affair at which her engagement to a son of the Johnsons, the original owners, was to be announced. With her she took her young sister.

"The Johnson boy immediately fell in love with the young sister – and the engagement was called off."

Eventually he married the younger girl, and his erstwhile fiancée became an old maid. Out of compassion they invited her to come to Gagetown and live with them. She accepted, then she found she couldn't stand seeing her sister in her former sweetheart's arms. She hanged herself in the closet of an upstairs bedroom.

A cold sense of foreboding came over Peggy di Carlo as the macabre story unfolded. Even before she asked, "Which bedroom?", she knew.

But that was only the start of the aging uncle's spooky memories.

"I was going to sleep in that bedroom one night many years ago," he said, "when to my surprise I saw a lady dressed in white walk into that closet. I thought it must be one of the girls in the house wanting to get some clothes. But no one came out again before I finally fell asleep."

Breathes Peggy di Carlo today, "It sure raised the goose pimples on me."

She surmises that her Aunt Margaret knew all along there was something supernatural about that bedroom.

"I remember she always gave that room to visiting priests," Mrs. di Carlo says. "And someone told me she asked Father Boyd of Petersville to bless it."

Understandably, Patricia Jenkins was interested when this latest jigsaw piece was passed on to her to fit into the puzzle of the old mansion's spectral history.

In the three years since I had spent time in Gagetown while writing the ghost book, I asked, had the presence been behaving pretty well?

"We've heard sounds – half a dozen times – but no one has seen anything."

What kind of sounds? Footsteps?

"No, like rustling of clothing when someone is walking. If you're in the living room, you look up expecting someone to come in, but no one appears.

"The sounds may come from upstairs, or, if you're in another part of the house, from the living room itself. Several people besides myself have heard them plainly."

Does the strange rustling upset visitors?

"No," replies Patricia Jenkins with her usual cheerfulness. "When they say, 'What's that I hear?' I say, 'Oh, just a guest going by.'"

And the presence *is* a guest, apparently, a permanent one.

When Ocean Flying Was in Rompers

Excitement ran high in the town of Shediac, and the reverberations were felt all over New Brunswick.

For there, riding at anchor in Shediac Bay on Northumberland Strait, were twenty-four gleaming Savoia-Marchetti flying boats, the transatlantic air armada led by Italy's bearded long-distance aviator Marshal Italo Balbo.

The year was 1933, and the excitement was not so much over the dashing marshal as what the mass flight portended – the approach of ocean passenger air service.

As we all knew in those days, flying the Atlantic was a nip-and-tuck affair, a tense long-jump from one shore to the nearest shore on the other side. So if Shediac Bay had attracted the Italians, why shouldn't it become an international air terminus?

No one dreamed that a generation later giant airliners would be unconcernedly flying from Vancouver over the roof of the world to Europe, and non-stop from Dallas to Hawaii, and Chicago to Tokyo.

Naturally New Brunswick in those days looked to the future with great expectations, because the province was definitely on the pioneers' migratory flyway route; early transoceanic daredevils were becoming as thick as seagulls over the Atlantic provinces.

Captain John Alcock and Lieutenant Arthur Whitten-Brown had made history for Britain in 1919 by coaxing their Vickers

Vimy bomber from Newfoundland to Ireland – the first non-stop Atlantic crossing.

In May, 1927, Charles Lindbergh flew low over the Maritimes en route to Paris on his epochal solo flight.

Even as he passed over, lumberjack crews were combing the New Brunswick forests on the chance that the transatlantic aircraft of French First World War ace Charles Eugene Jules Marie Nungesser and Francois Coli, who took off from Paris for New York twelve days before, had crashed in this region. No trace of them has ever been found.

The embryonic transatlantic air map was dotted with human tragedies, and no flier knew when he or she would be next to be marked on it with a cross. They were suspenseful days. It's hard to imagine now, but when a fuel-laden little plane lumbered off the runway to attempt an ocean crossing, it disappeared into the morning mists and into complete oblivion. It didn't carry wireless or radio – so it was farther out of touch with the world than today's spaceship circling the moon. People on the ground could only wait and hold their breath for twenty-four hours or thirty-four – or indefinitely. Even some freighters lacked wirelesses, so if one plucked a flier out of the sea it might be twelve days before it reached port and the news was flashed out.

It seemed in April 1928 that the crew of the German Junkers monoplane "Bremen" – Baron Gunther von Huenefeld, Captain Herman Koehl, pilot, and Irish co-pilot Colonel James Fitzmaurice – had shared the fate of Nungesser and Coli. They took off from Dublin for New York, and then, for days, just silence.

Suddenly came a report they had crash-landed on lonely Greenely Isle in the Straits of Belle Isle between Newfoundland and Labrador. A Saint John nurse, Greta Ferris, serving at a small cottage hospital of the Grenfell Mission at Forteau Inlet, harnessed up her five huskies and travelled by dogsled to the scene, got the story of how the aircraft had been forced down by lack of fuel and strong head winds in a blizzard and fog, and sent it by wireless from the Labrador coast via the Red Head Station in Saint John to her home newspapers. It was electrifying news to an anxious world.

Times-Globe city editor Joe Mooney, who loved a scoop, admitted afterward with a rueful grin: "I got so excited I lit a cigarette, blew out the match, and stuffed the cigarette in my pocket."

In the early 1930's came the deluge. Transatlantic aviators were almost getting in each other's propeller backwash.

Amelia Earhart was standing on the little Saint John airport tarmac, scanning the skies for a break in the weather as she got ready to go on to Harbour Grace and a date with destiny: she was to become not only the first woman to fly the Atlantic solo but also the record-holder for fastest crossing (fourteen hours, fifty-six minutes).

It was a time you'd expect frayed nerves, but the smiling boyish-looking aviatrix with the light tousled hair, who in her familiar tan suede jacket, khaki shirt and jodhpur-type breeches looked like a sister of Charles Lindbergh, was unfailingly cool, courageous and very considerate of onlookers who asked needless questions, like "What are you looking at?" When one said, "What do you think your chances are?" she replied offhandedly, "It's in the laps of the gods" – as any fool should have known.

A day or two later the intrepid young woman – then thirty-four and the wife of U.S. publisher George Palmer Putnam – set her crimson Lockheed down at Derry in northern Ireland. She had twenty dollars in her pocket and a copy of our morning *Telegraph-Journal*, the first newspaper to reach the British Isles the day after publication.

What most people didn't realize then – nor do they today – was that all those epic crossings were continuous hairbreath escapes from death. Not one had a completely clear-sailing flight into the azure blue horizon.

Lindbergh – as everyone knows by now from the TV re-enactments – nearly didn't make it; he was beset by emergencies time and again.

And listen to Amelia Earhart afterward:

"I wasn't really frightened, but it wasn't very pleasant when my exhaust manifold broke four hours out from Newfoundland, and bright red flames started shooting out by the side of the plane. If there had been a gas or oil leak it would have been too bad.

"Then to make matters worse, my altimeter broke – the first time in years of flying it happened to me. I was flying blind for fully five hours in darkness and rain, and the only thing to do was to get altitude. I started going in the direction I thought was up, and after a while the tachometer and I knew I was high enough."

Only three months later, in August, a tiny silver-gray Puss Moth plane dropped down into James Armstrong's blueberry patch in Pennfield Ridge, N.B., in a rainstorm. Out climbed a grease-smeared man in a big teddybear flying suit who enquired with British understatement of the startled farmer:

"I am all in. Do you mind if I leave my plane for the night?"

The casual aviator was James A. Mollison, who had just flown the Atlantic – the first man in history to make the wind-buffeted westward crossing alone.

You had to see his aircraft, the *Heart's Content*, to appreciate the magnitude of the feat.

It looked like a frail pipsqueak, the kind of weekend sports plane you used to see clustered around airports a generation ago.

It had only 120 horsepower, barely enough to lift its 170 gallons of petrol in taking off from Portmarnock, Ireland. Small wonder it was called "the flying gas tank." And the flight took thirty hours and fifteen minutes, a long ordeal for the pilot, who subsisted on nibbled barley sugar washed down by nips of brandy.

But the pilot was an exceptional man. A stalwart blond Scot, Jim Mollison was utterly confident, but cautious too; he carried twenty luck charms as a hedge. He called it the "toughest flight I ever made."

He had taken off in rain, flown through heavy fog, so his wet reception in New Brunswick was no surprise.

As in other successful Atlantic crossings, it was a cliff-hanger from start to finish.

"I was lucky," said the exhausted flier. "For hours at a stretch I flew through fog banks and rain. I couldn't see the water below me, and I didn't know whether the wind was switching and causing me to drift off my course. I never got above 5,000 feet."

Reporters brought him forty miles to the Saint John newspaper's office where he drank a cup of tea and munched on a sugar-coated bun. While photographers buzzed around he placed a transatlantic phone call to his famed aviatrix bride of only three weeks before, Amy Johnson, in London. Amy had been the first woman to fly from England to Australia.

Mollison sounded apologetic when he told her he didn't reach New York, but really could have made it if he wasn't so completely fagged out. "I still had ten gallons of petrol in my tanks." (Imagine trying to drive a medium-sized car today from Pennfield to New York on ten gallons. It would take at least thirty-six gallons.)

The whole scene was somehow unreal. If Jim Mollison had been an amateur actor made up for a church stage play, you'd have taken him to task right away – "Don't just put a discreet dab of grease on each cheek, put some on your nose and neck and other places! Walk staggery – you haven't slept for two days!"

But this was real life, and truth is sometimes stranger than fiction is permitted to be.

Being a grown-up twenty-one years old myself, I couldn't understand how an aging man of twenty-seven could possibly stand the prolonged pressure.

But I want you to know I played a part in the great transatlantic air beginnings. When Amelia Earhart's mentor, the celebrated Norwegian-American ocean flier Bernt Balchen, came to Saint John with Merion C. Cooper, producer of the documentary movie *Grass* (and later, *King Kong*), the City Council decided to tender them a surprise banquet. Balchen was embarrassed; he was wearing an open shirt. I lent him my tie. Whether I got it back I can't remember. But I had made my entry in the history books.

It seemed in fact that anybody who was anybody in aviation passed through Saint John: Igor Sikorsky, the helicopter inventor . . . Clarence Chamberlain, Ruth Nichols (who cracked up her plane in landing) . . . Danish ocean airmen Hillig and Hoiriis . . . the Flying Hutchinson family.

And then over the horizon in 1936 came that great looming cigar-shaped German dirigible *Hindenburg*, filling the sky so completely many people swore they could have reached up and touched it. Cows cringed, ducked and bolted. Everybody looking up was convinced the air leviathan lingered above the big dry dock plant, no doubt gathering intelligence for Hitler. Passengers staring out the portholes included former heavy-weight world champion boxer Max Schmeling.

Later, on a return trip in 1937, the dirigible was to plunge in flames at Lakehurst, New Jersey, carrying thirty-six out of the ninety-seven on board to a fiery death.

Understandably, Amelia Earhart is the personality remembered most vividly after all these years, even though in 1936 Jim Mollison crossed the Atlantic for an unprecedented fourth time.

She went on to other pioneering records, including the first flight by a woman from Hawaii to California.

And then, unbelievably, in 1937 –

With her navigator, Fred Noonan, she was on the last leg of a round-the-world attempt. Somewhere in the Pacific between New Guinea and Howlett Island they vanished. Scores of planes and ships scoured more than 200,000 square miles of ocean without a clue.

Was Amelia Earhart rescued by Japanese fishermen after coming down between two atolls, as one rumour said, and taken to Japan for questioning? Was she really spying for the United States on Japanese preparations for war?

Years later, an American doctor coming home from the Pacific brought a photo said to have been found on the body of a Japanese soldier. A white woman in the snapshot, who looked very much like Miss Earhart, was standing on a plane wing. Crowded around her were natives, with a Japanese soldier in the background. Nothing further has been learned.

Conceivably – just possibly – Amelia Earhart is still alive somewhere today, a permanent prisoner whose belated release would be too awkward for a foreign government to explain.

Those who met her in the early 1930's still think of her in a set image – an image fixed when the hands of the clock stopped – the all-American girl-next-door, a Doris Day who radiated a charm as fresh as daisies blowing in the field.

What is difficult, almost impossible, to grasp is that if she *is* alive, she is now a dear old lady in her eighties.

Mysterious Billy Smith

Into a smoke-bleary New Orleans boxing gym one day around 1890 sauntered a lad broad of shoulders, who looked about sixteen.

The original Jack Dempsey, the "Non-Pareil," middleweight champion of the world, was feinting, jabbing, dancing, bobbing, shadow-boxing in the centre of the ring.

"Isn't that Jack Dempsey?" the boy asked a bystander.

"Sure is," he replied. "But tough luck – he's got to defend the title in ten days, and he has no sparring partner."

The boy said, "I'll spar with him to help him out."

The man wandered over to an agitated onlooker who evidently was Dempsey's manager.

"There's a kid over here says he'll work out with Dempsey."

The manager promptly went to the boy. "Be here tomorrow afternoon." He never thought for a moment that the young fellow would show up.

But show up he did. He disdained the gear they offered "to protect your forehead." He said, "Give it to that monkey over there" – indicating Jack Dempsey.

The sparring match, watchers said, was a classic – a toe-to-toe whirlwind pummel-fest, in which the young stranger gave as good as he received.

Afterward Jack Dempsey came over and put an encouraging arm around the boy's shoulder.

"What's your name?"

"Billy Smith."

"Well, you're going to be the next welterweight champion of the world."

And he was. He started his twenty-one-year professional career in 1891 and won the title from Tom Williams two years later.

All through my newspaper days, from the 1920's on, I heard fantastic tales about this Mysterious Billy Smith from Saint John. But human memory gradually fades, and people die, and from 1950 on there had been hardly a whisper.

I enquired of a former boxing promotor, Jack McAllister, living in a retirement home. Happily, he knew a lot about the fighter, because he had files on practically every one of them, though his main preoccupation was the greatness of heavyweight champ Jack Dempsey, whom he knew. ("With two hands like his, he could make mincemeat out of these clowns like Joe Louis and Muhammad Ali.")

Born of Saint John parents while they were residing temporarily in Eastport, Maine, Billy Smith returned with them at two years and grew up in the rugged North End of the city. He learned early how to use his fists to defend himself against neighbourhood bullies – and thrived on it.

In short, Billy Smith was a hell-bent natural scrapper, a fighter who fought for the sheer joy of fighting.

"When he was a stripling of only ten or twelve," recollects Jack McAllister, "he went around town and sought out the best sluggers, men of 200 pounds, and took them on."

Heavy-necked, granite-jawed, with massive sinews that belied the graceful flexibility of his body, Billy Smith looked formidable even though he was only five feet eight inches tall and never got above 140 pounds.

But Billy could never be a model for the members of your local Boy Scout troop. He was, instead, a newsworthy phenomenon of his time – a terrific brawler whose sole obsession was to win, even if it meant foul punches, butting, holding by the neck, hitting after the bell. It was the code of the streets.

Which was doubtless why he held the debatable distinction of forfeiting more fights on fouls than any world champion in boxing history.

His professional record: Won, thirty-one; lost, fifteen; drew, twenty-eight.

Of the fifteen defeats, eleven were bouts lost on fouls.

Billy Roche, a leading U.S. referee, commented, "Of all the fighters I met in my life, Mysterious Billy Smith and Elbows McFadzen were the roughest and toughest. I managed both. Smith in the ring was as vicious as a trapped mountain lion – all strength and guts. In ordinary life he always had a chip on his shoulder, and heaven help anybody who knocked it off or even jarred it unintentionally."

This opinion was endorsed by another leading New York referee, "Patsy" Hanley, who coupled Mysterious Billy Smith's name with other great old-time stand-up welterweights, middleweights, and light heavyweights – Tommy Ryan, Kid McCoy, the original Joe Walcott. "It would be laughable to compare them with the fighters of today, they were so superior in every way."

"Smith," said Patsy Hanley, "was the wildest, fiercest rough-and-tumble fighter who ever lived. He had dynamite in both fists and a surprising grasp of science.

"What Smith would do to the current crop of welterweights, even the middleweights, would spin you around. He'd massacre the whole lot in one evening."

Personally, as a boxing fan, I'm glad I wasn't around in Mysterious Billy Smith's time – for I find watching a fifteen rounder on TV an exhausting experience, a too-long ordeal, if I'm cheering for my own favourite. When craggy-faced Yvon Durelle of Baie Ste. Anne, N.B., fought light-heavy champ Archie Moore for the world crown, I slipped off the edge of my chair and crashed on the living-room floor every time Yvon knocked Archie Moore to the canvas – all four times. Actually, I think, psychologically, symbolically, I was trying to help Archie Moore down. When Leon Spinks, making his bid for the heavyweight title, kept punching relentlessly through the fourteenth and fifteenth rounds to the end, but the first judge awarded the fight to Muhammad Ali, I shouted back angrily at the TV set.

So I'm happy not to have been there in 1891 when Mysterious Billy Smith, making his pro debut, was stopped – in the forty-ninth round.

After winning the world title in 1893, he lost it to Tommy Ryan the next year.

He regained the championship in 1896, lost it again to Rube Ferns in 1900.

But Mysterious Billy Smith is remembered by old-timers not because he lost so often on gutter tactics, not because he held the world title twice, but because he always could be relied on to give the fans a donnybrook of a fight.

Six of his most celebrated hammer-and-tongs battles were with the original Joe Walcott, the barrel-chested "Barbados Demon," who stood only five foot one but had extraordinary long arms, unbelievable stamina and awesome ability to punish as hard as he was punished. Walcott, one of the early great black fighters, eventually won the welterweight title in 1901, lost it in 1904, regained it in 1906.

But how did Billy Smith get the "Mysterious" handle?

Apparently a ring announcer, preparing to introduce him, once asked him his full name.

"Billy Smith," he answered.

The announcer looked at him dubiously. "Is that all?"

"Yes."

The man couldn't believe anyone had such a mundane name, so he publicly called him "Mysterious Billy Smith."

If he had only known, the announcer was right. Smith *had* changed his name to something he thought was more glamorous.

His original first name was Amos.

Life Begins at Fifty
(Or, the Incredible Dan Ross)

"*Ho, ho, ho, ho!* Here's a letter from little Jamie Saunders of Britain Street. He wants a train that runs on a track! Well, Jamie, old Santa will do his best, and I know you'll be happy with whatever I bring you on Christmas Eve."

How often I heard these glowing assurances delivered in a sonorous baritone! It was jolly old Saint Nick himself, holding forth over a Saint John radio station for Scovil Bros. department store (and incidentally for a few dollars for himself to buy groceries). He kept it up for two decades.

Matter of fact, by popular demand he still does a nostalgic CBC capsule performance as Santa every year, even though he hardly needs grocery money any more. He now reaps an annual income of reputedly well over $100,000 – which friends say also happens to be the approximate value of his lovely home in Saint John's suburbs overlooking the two-mile-wide Kennebecasis River.

He's Dan Ross, the most prolific author in the English language. He turns out a new novel every two weeks.

Withal, he's refreshingly modest. When he admits he once wrote a 75,000-word book, *Operating Room Nurse*, in six days, he explains seriously, "Of course, that was a special request."

He winces when someone introduces him at a banquet as "the man who has written more books than anybody else in the English language."

"I've written only between 300 and 400," he hastens to point out. "Others have written more. I've only written more books than anyone else *in the same space of time.*"

You see, Dan Ross isn't one of those precocious literary aspirants who started at nineteen. He didn't begin writing in earnest until he was in his fiftieth year.

As a youthful night city editor, I first knew him in the hungry thirties when he strolled into the newsroom every week with a brief item about that evening's performance of his little professional stage troupe. Sometimes it was a benefit for a Sons of England lodge, sometimes the Knights of Pythias, sometimes the ladies of the Loyal Orange Benevolent Association.

"How'd you do tonight?" I asked.

"Well, fair," he replied cheerfully. "We cleared $8.95. It may be even better tomorrow."

Which reflects the frightening tenacity and self-discipline he imposed on himself. At least it could be said in that era he outdid some frustrated Broadway producers who were going into the red $50,000 a week.

He credits that stage experience for his speed in book-writing: "It's made it possible for me to portray a book structurally."

Most of his output is the Gothic novel, a form of romantic suspense book about a lovely and innocent heroine in distress. But he writes also supernatural stories, romances, nurse dramas, detective yarns, westerns, historical novels.

Just in case his name doesn't ring all that familiarly to you, he writes not only as Dan Ross but also as Marilyn Ross, his second wife, who was a nurse attending his late first wife; as Dan Roberts, Leslie Ames, Clarissa Ross, Ruth Dorset, Ellen Randolph, Jane Daniels, Rose Dana, Rose Williams, Jane Rossiter, Tex Steele.

To say the spectrum of Dan Ross' writing is far-reaching is to understate it. A few years ago my wife and I were driving southward from New Brunswick through Connecticut and on the car radio we heard the author of *China Shadows* being interviewed for an hour on a Hartford radio station. The good-natured laughing writer sounded exactly like Dan Ross, yet I knew it couldn't be; he had never been to China. But, as I learned later, it was. He had done research on China for a detective series years ago. So now he had written a novel set in China. "After all," he said, "the story was laid in the China of 1840 or 1850. Who could be there?"

His hard-cover and soft-cover books flow out from eight United States publishers for markets in North America and two dozen countries abroad, from Norway to Hong Kong and Singapore. An average paperback edition is 750,000 copies. His total circulation so far: more than 25,000,000. For instance, one publishing company has exclusive rights to books by "Marilyn Ross." Three handle books by "Clarissa Ross." (Dan prefers his feminine pseudonyms for Gothic romances, as women readers seem to respond better to women writers.)

Between times he has found moments to write 600 short stories and a number of books based on ABC's television soap series *Dark Shadows* about a 175-year-old vampire; the books have had a circulation of more than eight million.

But he's not interested in television writing itself any more: "I've made my name in the novel field, so it wouldn't pay me. In TV I found I was working with so many people I had little control."

At home, working on his fortnightly novel, Dan Ross without a doubt wields complete control. He looks after his correspondence in the morning, and at eleven A.M. goes into voluntary solitary confinement. He secludes himself in a small soundproof basement room and sits down with a portable typewriter on his knees and begins churning out his daily 10,000 words.

After a four-hour stint, he surfaces at three P.M. and then goes underground again from four o'clock to seven, and once again from eight-thirty to midnight. Altogether it adds up to ten and a half hours a day, seventy-three and a half hours a week, so it's probably just as well he never joined a labour union.

Upstairs his wife Marilyn busily acts as test reader, first-version editor, researcher, nursing consultant, proofreader, secretary, and shield against interruptory visitors or phone calls.

"Without her," he admits, "I simply couldn't write the volume I do."

Obviously Marilyn is as dedicated to the daily marathon sprint as her husband. For recreational therapy between typing sessions they go for walks with their pet West Highland terrier Jolly. And anyway as Dan remarks, he doesn't really keep driving himself day and night: "I usually take twenty-four hours off between books." And − "to preserve my sanity" − they head every so often for Boston and New York, where the Rosses are familiar first-nighters at Broadway theatres and move in close-knit circles that include the leading stage luminaries of London and Manhattan. They entertain not only in New York but in Boston, where the Mugar Memorial Library of Boston University has established a permanent collection of Dan's personal papers and writings.

That's one of the paradoxical things about Dan Ross. At home he's known as only a fellow who used to be Santa Claus, and was supposed to have gone in for writing later, although few townsfolk can recall ever seeing his name on a book. When the Rosses periodically host a huge Rothesay party with a Boston combo alternating with a Saint John dance band − to mark his 200th book or his 300th − people shake their heads in puzzlement: How can a struggling author do it?

Another anomaly: He won't work for $8.95 a night any more. "I'm a professional," he says. "I write for money. I won't write a thing unless I get five dollars a word." Yet as the first president of the revised New Brunswick Branch, Canadian Authors' Association and an executive member since, he freely gave hundreds of hours to encourage would-be-writers.

No author is envious of Dan's income. For one reason, he's gregarious, helpful, and has the knack of laughing at his output. Because of his many pen-names, he calls himself "Canada's best-known unknown author." Also, his friends know his climb was no sudden stroke of luck: He laboured and studied relentlessly for many years.

Born in Saint John, the son of a railway investigator, W.E. Dan Ross began by writing high school plays. When his father died in 1937, he was left with $300 and a mother to look after. He studied drama at Greenwich Village's Provincetown Playhouse in New York, acted in summer stock in the United

States. Then he formed his Little Theatre group, which travelled the Maritime Provinces and, ironically, did better everywhere than in his home town.

During the Second World War he played in an entertainment unit, later operated a film distributorship. In the mid-1950's he studied writing at the University of Oklahoma, then launched himself into serious short story authorship – and made a net $500 in the first two years.

Not until Dan Ross was fifty, in 1962, was his first novel published, *Summer Stock*, based on his background in New England repertory. Its 3,500 copies at least paid production expenses.

Today no one realizes better than Dan Ross he has a tiger by the tail. He can't slow down, even though he'd like to, because he has too many commitments. There's always a deadline mocking him. And he's understandably proud of his reputation for never failing to deliver to a publisher on time.

"It's a race," he says. "You get locked in and can't escape."

One reason he'd like to taper off is that now, in his sixties, he's beginning to notice the strain.

"A writer has to feel all the emotions of all his characters in every chapter," he points out. "It wears you down mentally and physically. I acquired an ulcer from punishing myself; I could tell how intensely I felt each situation by how the ulcer reacted."

Another yardstick, which he cites quite straightforwardly and a little sadly, confirms that he's decelerating: "I used to be able to write a novel in two weeks quite easily. Now I find I'd rather take three weeks."

If you drop in at Dan Ross' home – and if you luckily catch him between writing grinds – he's a disarmingly jovial host who'd obviously much rather talk shop than work, if he could spare the time. He wears a turtle-neck sweater, a bright wine-red corduroy jacket, casual slacks. He's reached the stage where he can afford to be himself. If he wants to take his dog everywhere with him, he does. Once he flew to Toronto for a national TV interview, and to my surprise on the screen at home he appeared with his nose bandaged. I thought he had been mugged. He explained to me afterward: When he got to Toronto and went to take his pet out of the air-freight kennel, the dog was so keyed up it bit him on the nose. So, naturally, he went on the national network with his nose taped.

Why does he stay in New Brunswick? Not just because his New York agents advise him to ("You're out of the endless cocktail circuit, and away from crazy autograph hounds"), but also because he likes the people and what he calls "the slower pace of life."

If his is a slower pace of life, it would be interesting to see what a busy pace is.

Will there continue to be a huge mass market for his type of writing?

"The kids in the United States aren't reading," Dan Ross replies. "They can't read. The number of people reading is getting less every year. U.S. book publishers are greatly concerned. They're trying to develop different kinds of books that will catch school kids early."

You don't ask him what his chief regret about writing is, if any, because you may discern it anyway. Dan Ross is well aware that his fame rests entirely on being what he calls a hack, a writing freak, a literary factory, a human production line. But some critics have put in a word for his writing style – "a good deal better than the average for the bestselling novels of recent years," said one. Comments Dan wistfully, "Some of it really isn't so bad."

One thing keeps puzzling the visitor: "You keep a portable typewriter on your knee ten and a half hours a day – don't you get numb legs?"

"No," he replies seriously, "but I wear out a lot of pants."

It's a long, long way back to the chill wintry days when Dan Ross eked out a paltry living by acting as Santa. Perhaps that's one reason why he still exercises his vocal chords in the role every Christmas – to remind himself how lucky he is, and how fickle is a fate that now enables him to go *ho-ho-hoing* all the way to the bank.

The Suicide
of the *Jervis Bay*

Since time immemorial, the salt waters that lap the Atlantic Provinces' shores have been churned by bloody battles, although the history books seldom mention them.

In the early 1600's, the great Micmac chief Membertou led hundreds of war-painted braves in a huge flotilla of birchbark canoes across the swells of the Bay of Fundy to join with the Maliseets and paddle down to Maine to avenge the death of Chief Pennoniac, who had been slain by the Armourchiquois while guiding the French explorers de Monts and Champlain. In a sanguinary fray at Saco, Membertou's invaders killed Chief Bessabez and many of his deputy chiefs.

A few years afterward Charles de la Tour enlisted the aid of Puritan ships from Boston to break the naval siege of his Saint John fortress by rival seigneur d'Aulnay Charnisay and chase the enemy vessels across the fifty-mile-wide bay to Port Royal.

Later, Captains Bonaventure and d'Iberville at the helms of their warships were to duel constantly with English rivals in the bay outside Saint John harbour.

And in 1745 a rag-tag shuffling seaborne army of New England volunteers – farmers, clerks, lumberjacks, schoolboys, barroom sots – performed the seemingly miraculous feat of capturing Fortress Louisbourg in Cape Breton, the "Dunkirk of the North." The stronghold was given back to France in a subsequent treaty, and in 1758 a stronger New England force subdued Fort Louisbourg all over again.

Two years later a climactic encounter in the struggle for North America took place in the Bay of Chaleur: the destruction of a smaller French force by Commodore "Foul Weather Jack" Byron in the Battle of the Restigouche near today's city of Campbellton, N.B. The course of Canadian history might have been entirely changed if the French squadron had smashed through the British blockade to enter the St. Lawrence River and recapture Quèbec.

The U.S. Revolutionary War and the War of 1812 saw interminable skirmishes between British warships and American privateers in the Bay of Fundy.

Unquestionably one of the most memorable moments for the Maritimes in those years was the triumphant entry into Halifax harbour of the British frigate H.M.S. *Shannon* with the captured frigate U.S.S. *Chesapeake* in tow on June 6, 1813.

It had been a classic battle to the death, the day the two frigates clashed off Boston. British Captain Sir Philip Bowes Vere Broke was spoiling for a ship-to-ship match – particularly since the Royal Navy, discounting the gunnery skill and seamanship of the upstart Americans, had been defeated in five previous single-ship fights.

He even sent a personal challenge ashore, promising that no other British warship would be within sailing distance. It is doubtful, however, whether Captain James Lawrence of the *Chesapeake* ever received the message.

A gala atmosphere of anticipation pervaded Boston. Everyone wanted to enjoy the battle. Yachts and pleasure boats were readied to carry wealthy thrill-seekers out to the best vantage points to watch – even as, years afterward, elegant gentlemen and their ladies in silk and lace finery rode coaches out to see the imminent Battle of Bull Run in the U.S. Civil War, only to be shocked by the ear-splitting din of shot and shell and revolted by the sight of mangled arms and legs flying through the air.

The naval drama itself was short and gory; it lasted little more than twelve minutes. The British ship immediately took the initiative, raking the *Chesapeake* with fire; then an explosion rocked the U.S. frigate amidships; as the warships grappled, sword-swinging Royal Navy boarders swarmed on to the decks of the enemy and in moments it was all over. Among those fatally wounded was the *Chesapeake's* Captain Lawrence. The British did such an effective job, in fact, they even by mistake blasted away one of their own officers and six sailors who in error raised the stars and stripes above the British ensign on the captured ship. Onlookers on U.S. yachts, to their astonishment, saw the *Chesapeake* sail away for Halifax in the wake of the *Shannon*.

In the strange courtesy of war – strange to civilians, at least – Royal Navy officers who had leaped aboard the *Chesapeake*, swords flashing, slashing right and left, slaughtering all who resisted, wore black mourning crepe armbands as they followed the casket of Captain Lawrence in Halifax, to the accompaniment of muffled drums, minute guns, the falsetto notes of boatswain's pipes, the melancholy dirge of a naval band, as if sorry to see him go. In naval etiquette this was a tribute to a courageous foe.

Probably nobody in Halifax realized more what it was like to live in a great naval bastion than Reverend Mr. Stanser, rector of St. Paul's. First, to the chagrin of the British authorities, he was seized by a press-gang who thought he was a mere passer-by and intended to make him a seaman on a man-o'-war. And then, on Whitsunday, June 6, he had just started his sermon when word reached the congregation that the *Shannon* was sailing into port with the *Chesapeake* as a prize. As the news was whispered around, people left the church in twos and threes and sprinted for the harbourfront, followed by more and more worshippers . . . and then the choir galloping in their black gowns . . . and not long after, the clergy, and Reverend Mr. Stanser himself, who didn't want to miss anything.

In both the First and Second World Wars, Canadian warships and German U-boats had brushes off the Atlantic shores – but this story happens to deal with a naval exploit far from our coastline.

Saint John people felt a special affinity for the armed merchant cruiser H.M.S. *Jervis Bay*, a converted Australian freighter of 14,000 tons, even though the rallying point for Second World War convoys was Halifax, commonly referred to in officially censored news despatches as "An East Coast Canadian Port" – so often, in fact, that in England Lord Halifax became known colloquially as "Lord East Coast Canadian Port."

This personal interest was due to the fact that the eighteen-year-old *Jervis Bay* had spent several months in the summer of 1940 being refitted in the Saint John dry dock, and people around the city and suburbs had made warm friends of Captain E.S. Fogarty Fegan and his Royal Navy officers and crew.

A forty-nine-year-old Irishman from Ballinlouty in County Tipperary, the son of a rear admiral, Captain Fegan was a sailor's sailor. A wartime member of the crew, Robert Squires of Saint John West, recalls him admiringly as "a good, fair skipper – the sort that knew a sailor when he saw one." When the war broke out he was serving in the Naval College of Australia at Jervis Bay.

The captain's job was to protect convoys on the North Atlantic run from Halifax as far as Iceland. No one knew better than he that if his improvised warship had the misfortune to meet a German pocket battleship armed with eleven-inch guns hurling 750-pound shells, he would have to "close" the enemy and take a merciless pounding, like a doomed boxer against the ropes, to buy time for the convoy to scatter. His erstwhile liner was hopelessly outgunned.

"You wouldn't believe it," reminisces Robert Squires, "but our six-inch guns were made in 1899 and 1900 for the Boer War."

On November 5, eight days out of Halifax, on the *Jervis Bay's* third convoy trip after leaving Saint John, the nightmare came true.

The flock of thirty-eight ships was 250 miles from the coast of Greenland on a dull cloudy day when at 4:50 P.M. an ominous speck was seen on the horizon.

Immediately the *Jervis Bay* challenged the stranger by signalling it. The answer: A salvo of shells at extreme range.

One of the first targets was the 17,000-ton passenger liner *Rangitiki*.

The speck on the horizon was the pocket battleship *Admiral Scheer*, ten miles astern.

Under Captain Fegan's orders, the *Jervis Bay* got up steam, raced ahead and then turned in a wide arc, so that it could come down the line of the convoy with guns blazing at the Nazi sea raider while laying a smoke screen to conceal the merchant ships, which were fleeing by prearranged signal in the gathering darkness.

So 255 men, including a group of twenty Canadian trainees, headed into the jaws of death as surely as the Charge of the Light Brigade.

Because the *Jervis Bay* was fast narrowing the gap between them, the battleship had to concentrate its bombardment on the British vessel to destroy it before its smaller guns could find the mark.

After only fifteen minutes, the *Jervis Bay* was a smashed hulk. The engines were silenced by a direct hit; the battle flag fluttered to the deck and a seaman lashed it to the railing facing the *Admiral Scheer*; the bridge was splintered, the steering gear blasted away, one gun after another vanished with its crew in an explosive flash. As one survivor recalled, "It was an inferno – flying shell and flame all over the place."

For a whole hour the systematic battering, the grisly hammer blows, went on – and the wonder is that anyone came through it. Robert Squires' station was at No. 3 gun in the after-well deck; that gun was almost immediately knocked out of action by a shell that pierced the hull just below. He then helped carry the wounded into the sick bay – and another shell exploded in the sick bay, putting the wounded out of their suffering.

The *Jervis Bay* began to settle by the stern at the end of the hour, and the order to abandon ship was given. The last view anyone had of Fogarty Fegan was a mutilated figure of a man, one arm torn off, staggering from one part of the flaming bridge to another, shouting orders to his officers and men.

The *Jervis Bay's* remaining guns were still firing when, after three hours, the brave ship at last up-ended and disappeared beneath the frigid greenish-grey waves.

When the survivors looked for lifeboats, there were none. All had been shot to pieces. They tilted two life-rafts and slid them into the water, and launched a small jollyboat.

But the German warship began firing into the water around the sinking ship, and many men on the rafts hit by shrapnel tumbled into the rising seas.

"Do you think the German captain intentionally tried to kill the survivors?" I asked Robert Squires.

"Yes."

"Isn't that unusual in war?"

He shrugged, but declined to be bitter.

"In every war there are always good commanders and bad commanders on both sides."

The ordeal of the survivors was not yet over. After the able-bodied had piled the eighty wounded men in the middle of the largest raft, they themselves hung on to the lifelines around the raft.

The wind was approaching sixty-mile-an-hour gale intensity, the ocean now turbulent. Alternately the heavily laden raft would ride the crest of a wave, then plunge into the trough.

"When the raft went down, it took your breath away," Mr. Squires recollected. "The men jumped to their feet as the seas swept over, and the raft often flipped upside down, trapping many wounded underneath. Another few hours and no one would have survived."

By great good fortune the Swedish freighter *Stureholm*, rather than scrambling to safety, was circling about looking for anyone from the *Jervis Bay* still living. By next morning it had picked up sixty-five – all that were left of the original 255.

Said Captain Sven Olander, "They did so well for us that I didn't like to leave. It was glorious. Never will I forget the gallantry of that British captain sailing forward to meet the enemy."

Epilogue:

Lord Haw-Haw chortled on the German radio beamed at Britain next day, "There were no survivors."

Winston Churchill paid tribute to this "forlorn and heroic action," which had not scored a hit on the *Admiral Scheer* but had given the convoy so much priceless time that thirty-four out of thirty-eight vessels escaped.

Royal Navy officers reported the valour of the Canadians aboard was "a wonderful example of the courage and spirit of the Canadian navy."

Captain Fogarty Fegan's sister was presented with the Victoria Cross, Britain's highest bravery-in-action award, in her brother's memory.

Surviving British officers did their predictably typical best to downplay their experience. Said Paymaster-Lieutenant J.G. Sargeant, visiting friends in Rothesay, N.B.: "November the fifth is 'fireworks day' in England and we certainly had fireworks that day."

In Saint John East a twelve-foot monument was erected in 1941, with an illustrative bas-relief copper plate, to honour the heroic exploit.

The Saint John East branch of the Royal Canadian Legion renamed itself Jervis Bay Memorial branch.

Robert Squires, born in Hull, England, married a Saint John girl he had previously met. But the icy North Atlantic ordeal had taken its toll: he was invalided home to England in 1942 suffering from acute arthritis. They returned to Canada in 1944, and for many years until retirement Squires worked as a stationary engineer in Saint John.

And in April 1945, the pocket battleship *Admiral Scheer* was bombed and sunk by Royal Air Force Lancasters at Kiel naval base.

The Biggest Frog
in the World

The atmosphere was hushed, sombre, and awesomely dignified in the Law Library of the New Brunswick Justice Building. Black-gowned young lawyers hovered silently about, looking up tomes of writs, torts, binding injunctions, and early English statutes.

I was relieved that no one asked me what I was doing in this Fredericton referral centre of age-old jurisprudence.

I wanted to see about a frog.

Fortunately, the authority I intended to consult was a kindred spirit. A silver-haired retired gentleman of modest height, quiet-spoken and courtly in manner, retired plant pathologist Dr. Donald J. MacLeod was the associate law librarian. He also was one of the best-informed persons anywhere on the celebrated Coleman Frog, which now implacably looks out on the world from a glass case in the York-Sunbury Museum not far away at Officers' Square, off Queen Street in Fredericton.

It weighed, we are assured, forty-two pounds in its prime and measured three feet from nose-tip to rump.

Dr. MacLeod took me aside to a desk, out of the lawyers' hearing. "Just what did you want to know?"

"Are there really people," I said, "who believe in the Coleman frog, and seriously think that the stuffed exhibit in the museum was once actually the biggest frog in the world?"

He seemed taken aback. "Why, of course! Just ask practically anybody in Fredericton."

Then he told me the strange story, from an insider's vantage point. "Long before I came here in 1924 from Ontario," he said, "I heard about this frog from an uncle who travelled a lot and always stayed at the Barker House when he was in Fredericton."

The first thing Dr. MacLeod did, when he was sent to New Brunswick to take charge of the Dominion Plant Pathological Laboratory, was to go over to the Barker House to see the famous mounted frog reposing amidst the palm fronds.

The proprietor of the Fredericton hotel, Fred Coleman, also owned a summer guest hotel at Killarney Lake, only about four or five miles out the Killarney Road.

"It was a small lake," Dr. MacLeod reminisced, "not much more than a pond."

But in the lake Mr. Coleman had discovered a gigantic frog. And it was surprisingly approachable. He started feeding it treats, especially fresh-baked bread and buttermilk; and the frog loved them and kept growing.

Their friendship endured for years. A few people sniffed that Fred Coleman was ingratiating himself with the frog by swilling it with Scotch, gin and rum, although no one ever reported hearing the frog hiccuping from the rum, only chugarumming.

Guests at the Barker House in Fredericton helped vary the fare by taking June bugs and fireflies to Killarney Lake to toss to the hostel's pet.

Not that the frog always gratefully received the handouts. Like some people he got cranky at times when he thought well-wishers didn't bring him enough, and then he sulked in the lake depths.

In a few days he would surface again and Mr. Coleman would be patiently waiting with tasty tidbits.

However, in 1885, as it inevitably had to, it happened. Some greedy frustrated anglers dynamited a pool in Killarney Lake to kill trout – and with the fish they raised the hulk of a great lifeless frog.

Fred Coleman, inconsolable, had a taxidermist mount the famous frog for display in the Barker House.

That's the story accepted by a host of believers in Fredericton. They will readily cite you statistics about African frogs that grew to mammoth proportions.

But a few discordant voices keep saying a travelling salesman from New York came to Fredericton in the early days looking for lodging, and he carried with him a stuffed frog, or a reasonable facsimile, in a sealed glass case to publicize a patent remedy warranted to take the croakiness out of your throat.

Another report was that Mr. Coleman chanced to notice in a Boston store window a big stuffed frog in a sealed glass case, and he bought it to place in the Barker House lobby as a reincarnation of his departed friend.

On what did Dr. MacLeod base his own view?

"First," he said, "away back years ago we learned from Coleman's own son there actually was a pet frog. I heard that after the frog died, sympathetic people told Fred Coleman, 'You should get another.' But to my knowledge he never did. I tend to believe his version, even if he had the reputation of being a fellow who told great stories and believed them himself."

For a while after Mr. Coleman's death and the demolishing of the venerable Barker House under the wrecking-ball, the frog vanished from human ken.

"Finally," said Dr. MacLeod, "some ladies got wind of a rumour that Mrs. Coleman had the frog in Lincoln."

Mrs. Coleman was the only living charter member of the York-Sunbury Historical Society. So Dr. MacLeod went out to the Fredericton suburb two or three times to see her on behalf of the York and Sunbury Museum.

"She was a very gracious lady. She believed the original story implicitly. At first she demurred about letting the society put the frog on display, because she was afraid people wouldn't believe it was real and would only ridicule it. She pointed out that her husband believed completely in the authenticity of the frog, because he had told her so.

"Some time later she consented, on the stipulation we were to believe too and not present the frog in such a way as to belittle it in the minds of others. We made that promise."

Always prowling in the background, of course, are pragmatic skeptics just itching for a chance to prove the frog isn't a freak but a plastic-coated fake.

"I had a letter from a man in Toronto who asked if he could come down here and open the case," Dr. MacLeod remarked. "I said no, it was hermetically sealed, and opening it might affect the contents – and in any event it would be a shame to spoil a good story."

So everybody is welcome to come and look – but debunkers please stay away. True Frederictonians will never believe there is anything bogus about their pet frog, nor do they want to hear any outlander suggest such a thing.

And if you happen to be looking some day through the glass case at the enormous staring creature – with head and back and legs as murky green as the slime in a lake, and an immense chin down to its belly as creamy as yellow water lilies – and if you imagine that lurking around the corners of the mouth is a trace of a smile, perhaps you'd better believe that, too.

How I Became a University Benefactor for Four Dollars

We got a wonderful antique bargain!

The classified ad in the evening paper said, "Selling Out Contents of Large Germain Street Flat, including Old Furniture."

So my wife and I hurried there, because she always wanted one of those lovely plain old mahogany picture frames with sides four or five inches wide to put a large mirror in.

We bought a living-room carpet, but didn't see an old frame anywhere.

Just as we were walking down the stairs to leave, suddenly there it was! A glowing mahogany frame, about three and a half feet high, containing a picture too faint even to see in the hallway gloom.

We asked the lady how much she wanted for it.

"Oh, four dollars," she said after a moment's thought. "It came safely through the Great Saint John Fire of 1877, you know. But do me one favour: if you're not going to keep the picture, wait till you get home to throw it away. I've got enough mess here already."

We were only too happy to oblige. Even then, a generation ago, four dollars was reasonable for such a hard-to-find heirloom.

I stood the big picture – a sketch of an old church, in delicate tints – against the wall of our living room and turned the floor lamp to spotlight it.

For some reason I loved that picture. It fascinated me. Of course, the frame was too large to use in our apartment for anything except a mirror, but I hated to put the picture itself in the garbage barrel.

Not until the third day did I notice there was faint inch-high script-lettering below the bottom of the colour sketch. It said:

The Proposed Christchurch Cathedral, Fredericktown, New Brunswick.

I was startled. Fredericktown was the long-ago spelling of Fredericton. "Proposed" meant "not built yet." It took only a phone call to find out from the New Brunswick Museum that the cathedral was completed in 1853 – so the picture was obviously older than that.

The museum man was interested. "Are the colours in the picture pink, blue, and gold?"

"Yes. Why?"

"Because" – excitedly – "that sounds like a very rare picture, a stone engraving printed in England about 1825 and tinted by hand. Christchurch Cathedral, as you may be aware, is a very distinguished old church."

This was true. Modelled after St. Mary's at Snettisham, Norfolk, England, Christchurch was the first new cathedral foundation on British soil since the Norman Conquest of 1066. It has, among many historical attractions, a resident ghost and an ancient unorthodox clock that was the test-run timepiece for Big Ben in London's Parliament Buildings.

He asked, "Could you bring it to the museum to let us see it?"

I lugged the picture under my arm, trying to keep the frame from bumping the ground, on to a bus and up the long wide steps to the museum.

"That's it!" the curator cried. "Look, it's exactly the same as ours – the only one we know of in existence – in the Canadiana collection of Dr. J. Clarence Webster of Shediac!"

They *were* similar, the only slight difference being in the colouring.

"That's because they were hand-tinted," explained our friend.

I asked, "How much is my picture worth?"

He shrugged. "Whatever anyone wants to pay for it – any price! Christchurch Cathedral doesn't have one; there is no such picture in Fredericton."

Then a dazzling light hit me –

Lord Beaverbrook was arriving next week! He made a homecoming visit to the Miramichi and Fredericton every spring and fall. As life chancellor of the University of New Brunswick, he was its benefactor to the tune of millions of dollars. He knew me well, as I had been airmailing him weekly news clippings for seventeen years. (He enjoyed this arrangement. An old boyhood friend in Newcastle would break a leg, an item would appear in the local paper, and four days later would come a letter from His Lordship in London: "I'm extremely sorry to hear about your right leg." The recipient was astounded. "That man is incredible. He must be psychic!")

Naturally, I started calculating. Wouldn't a picture so rare be worth $1,000? Or, being priceless, why not $5,000? The more I thought about it, the higher it soared. After only half an hour I was a rich man.

Lord Beaverbrook, I should point out, was tremendously admired in New Brunswick, where he grew up. Most people elsewhere undoubtedly thought of him as a controversial phenomenon, the leading British (and world) newspaper publisher, a financier, political king-maker, the minister of aircraft production in the Second World War who miraculously kept Spitfires streaming out of bomb-scarred factories to turn the tide in the Battle of Britain.

New Brunswickers always looked at him as one of themselves, a Miramichi boy who made good – "the barefoot boy," he called himself with a bit of artistic licence – and they marvelled at the unstinting generosity of his multi-million-dollar gifts of scholarships, university residences, auditoriums, gymnasiums, rinks, art galleries, town halls, theatres to his old home province.

But to me, as a newspaperman, "the Lord" was something

else. When I marvelled, it was mainly because of his writings – crisp, incisive, cleverly honed phrases – in the numerous books he authored. His seemingly easy facility didn't come easily; he laboured at it, polished it relentlessly. Once I visited his élite hotel suite in Saint John and found the carpet so littered with crumpled notes it looked as if the ceiling was snowing popcorn balls. He was writing an address to give at Dalhousie University convocation in Halifax, and was agonizing over it.

And whenever he arose to speak, Beaverbrook completely dominated the audience. His vocal timbre and enunciation reminded you of his old friend Churchill. He would lead up to the climax of an anecdote, pause in the pregnant silence – then deliver the punchline and bring laughter and applause crashing around him like a tidal wave. I heard an American professor once utter to a colleague the ultimate accolade: "His timing is better than Bob Hope's."

So here I was with my wife at the door of the suite, my arms aching from the struggle with the huge picture, and visions of kegs of gold coins dancing in my head.

"Come in!" amiably bellowed the short nut-brown man, who held in his hands the glass container from an old blender. He was making cocktails. "Do come in and make yourself at home, please!"

He started the blender. The racket was as deafening as a cement-mixer.

Conversation was impossible; but Beaverbrook could rise above it. "MEAD!" he roared, almost lifting me off my chair, and the valet came running to serve the cocktails.

"Atrocious!" was the first word His Lordship spoke when the din suddenly ceased. "They're charging me seven dollars a day for a refrigerator in my suite. Atrocious!"

That was a characteristic I noticed not only in Lord Beaverbrook but in other enormously wealthy people. They didn't mind writing a cheque for a few millions to some worthy cause, but they reacted violently when they thought someone was taking advantage of them – even a few cents' worth – just because they were rich and fair game.

As for his roaring: The erstwhile Barefoot Boy, a son of the Presbyterian manse at Newscastle, was without doubt a thunderous personality. But he had also a gentle side – almost a feminine compassion, as one of his associates once remarked – and he could be unbelievably thoughtful. And he possessed an extraordinary knack of inspiring students and others to aim higher merely by expressing absolute confidence in their potential.

"Well, what have we got here?" he was demanding, looking at the big picture, and I came back to reality with a start.

"Oh, it's a picture," I stammered. "Christchurch Cathedral – an 1825 stone engraving, the only one of its kind outside the Webster Collection. . . . I acquired it. . . . I thought you would like to present it to the University of New Brunswick."

Lord Beaverbrook, if nothing else, was a lightning thinker.

He didn't wait for me to mention money.

"That I shall!" he exclaimed. "I shall present it in *your* name, and you shall become a benefactor of the university!"

I was stunned. While I still stood there, tongue-tied, he took the huge framed picture from under my arm; I wasn't quite sure what had happened.

Six months later, when UNB held its Spring Encaenia exercises in Fredericton, I saw it once more.

As the academic procession was breaking up after the graduation Lord Beaverbrook in his huge floppy cap and resplendent colourful robes, recognized us.

"You'd like to see the picture," he announced. "Come with me!"

We drove up the hill to the old library, and His Lordship hurried in first and spoke with the curator.

Both of them hastened up the stairs to the second floor and entered a big room. We heard a lot of commotion.

Several minutes later Lord Beaverbrook descended the stairs and said, almost with a sigh of relief: "You can come up now." For some reason it reminded me of how, when my Great-Aunt Charlotte came to call and we saw her from the window, we scrambled to get her mother's severe tintype portrait on the wall.

There, in the gallery of the university's honoured paintings, sure enough, was my 1825 stone engraving in its beautiful mahogany frame bordered by tiny gold beads on the inside.

Underneath was a card inscribed with my name as the donor, a benefactor of the university.

It was nice to look at.

I didn't mind losing the picture, I should explain. I couldn't have used it anyway.

But for some reason which I can't quite figure, I did mind losing my good four-dollar bargain frame.

The Reluctant Folk-singer

Aging Theophile Bourgeois, a tanned farmer with snowy bangs cut straight across his forehead, didn't want to get up and sing.

Anyone could see that.

A wrinkled hand kept brushing away the entreaties of the two laughing women trying to coax him off his kitchen chair. He was good-naturedly smiling but shaking his head as if remonstrating, "I'm a poor singer" or "I don't know any words."

It was a shame, I thought, the way they kept pestering the nice old fellow. I said so to the Acadian merchant I was visiting on the Petitcodiac River near Moncton.

"Oh, he's dying to sing!" replied my friend. "He's the best around here; he knows all the old songs. But you see, he can't sing unless he's coaxed. That's the old rule, the etiquette, you might say."

"But he *is* being coaxed."

"Not enough yet. Just watch."

The two persistent ladies must have tried to persuade him at least three times before the grandfatherly farmer at last stood up shyly and, as his listeners arranged their chairs in a circle, shuffled around to the back of his chair. Grasping the wooden top in bony fingers, he lowered his head for a few moments as if in meditation or prayer.

I thought he'd forgotten either the words or the melody, or both.

Suddenly he cleared his throat with a loud harrumph and, in a surprisingly robust voice, burst into song. The words were completely unintelligible to me, as I didn't understand French, and I couldn't detect any melodic pattern in the music, which was apparently sung in the same haunting five-tone scale heard in venerable English ballads at Newcastle's Miramichi Folksong Festival.

Talk about modesty! When the old boy finished, he walked around and sat himself down on the chair after saying *"Excusez-moi"*; he seemed to be asking pardon for giving such a poor performance.

Later I met Charlotte Cormier, then folklore curator in the Centre of Acadian Studies at the University of Moncton, and discovered that Theophile Bourgeois' backwardness in coming forward was all part of traditional Acadian ritual – the coaxing, the standing behind the chair, the gaze lowered in thought, the clearing of the throat, even the apology.

"And did you notice," she said, "that the old people just 'speak' the last line instead of singing it? That goes away back into antiquity."

Actually what I was noticing was the marked similarity between English and Acadian folk-song customs in New Brunswick. Both include ballads dating back seven centuries or more – brought over from the old homeland and passed down unchanged through generations by word-of-mouth. Both English and Acadian singers are usually unaccompanied, and stand with their arms hanging slack at their sides like Irish dancers. And both simply speak the last line as they quickly walk away.

For several summers I've attended the Miramichi festival – that uniquely exuberant celebration whose packed audiences may be hilariously whooping, hollering, and foot-stomping one minute and, in the next, wiping away a stray tear as heart-rending lines are sung about an obdurate father slamming the door on a wayward daughter with a freezing babe in her arms; about a raging forest fire sent by God as retribution for people's sins; about a guileless Prince Edward Island boy killed in a log jam; about shipwrecks and unrequited love and cruel mortgage-foreclosers.

Time-tested tear-jerkers include "goodnight songs," moralistic melodies supposedly written by condemned convicts about to be hanged – very profitable fast sellers when street urchins hawked them around the waiting gallows a century and more ago.

As for real antiquity, there's "The Old Beggar Man," a song dating from the Crusades – about a long-lost lover returning home to England – and assorted other ancient melodies adapted to new words describing Miramichi tragedies.

Although the undemonstrative singing stance of a Miramichi balladeer, without gestures, may seem monotonous, you should always be prepared for jolting surprises – for instance when several members of the audience suddenly feel inspired to dash up the stairs to the platform and do a step-dance, or yodel; or when a banjoist and pianist start playing along, or the singer finishes up with a falsetto "Whoo-pee!"; or ageless old Paul Kingston thinks it's a timely moment to blow blasts on his birch-bark moose-calling horn, which always brings a rousing ovation.

The audience is usually made up of three elements. First, the Miramichi people, who hang on every word, every intonation, every inflection of the singer – every little nuance – because although few know the big technical terms for such things, they know an outstanding performance from instinct and upbringing. They're like discriminating Met opera buffs who can appreciate the same arias over and over again.

Then there are the casual tourist visitors from the cities whose musical understanding doesn't go beyond the Lawrence Welk TV show, who yawn at the endless length of the Miramichi songs and shudder at the grammar and occasional lack of refinement:

But the captain told him for to go
  where water will not freeze

or,

So young lads, take my advice
  And look at your girl twice;
They are all out to fool a poor garson.

Pull their leg and pull their hair
And make sure she's all there;
  By the bright light of the silvery moon.

And finally there are the scholarly musical researchers and critics from all over North America, with their expensive tape recorders.

Listen to two of them talking about the Miramichi ballads.

One is earnestly holding forth about caesuras, time-signatures, compound metres, gapped scales, binary and triple organizations.

Just as enthusiastically the other is expounding on melismas, parlandos, microtones, elongated fermatas, hexachordal and tetrachordal variances and the Scotch snap, which is evidently not a quick nip.

It's almost enough to make the bewildered TV-tuned city visitor think that perhaps the Miramichi people know more about music than he thought.

One eminent musical authority, fascinated by the custom of merely speaking the last line, said he could locate this only in New Brunswick and the nearby northeastern United States, and also in Australia. Apparently it was an old English custom that had died out in the homeland and had been perpetuated in faraway former colonies.

But as I learned subsequently, Acadian folk-singers follow the same strange procedure, so it may have been general in north Europe centuries ago.

Inevitably, because of the public attention generated by the annual festival, Miramichi folk-songs have become widely known. It was Lord Beaverbrook, a former Newcastle boy, who in 1947 launched the late Dr. Louise Manny on an exhaustive quest for authentic old come-all-ye's – thus named because in woods camps the opening line was always "Come all ye jolly lumbermen and listen unto me."

Sitting in an old rocker at her Newcastle home a few years ago, Dr. Manny recalled she was skeptical about the whole thing at the outset – she didn't think many such ballads still existed. Beaverbrook was insistent, however, and his enthusiasm was contagious. He tossed off the names of several songs for a starter – including his own favourite, "The Jones Boys," who worked day and night but couldn't make their gosh-darned sawmill pay. And he reminded her to be sure to get "Hail Storm, Black Tom," which he claimed the Americans stole and revived as "It Ain't Gonna Rain No Mo'."

Some day, perhaps, the Acadians will have a yearly folk-song festival, too. Certainly, due to the unceasing labours of Charlotte Cormier and other modern researchers, the foundations have been laid.

Totally devoted to preserving Acadian culture, this attractive brunette young woman has collected 15,000 different items on cassette tapes, not only age-old folksongs – "They go back," she said, "as far as 1292" – but also folktales, legends, meteorological knowledge, fishing techniques, jokes, recipes, medicines, details about costumes and dances, anything, in fact, that pertains to the Acadians.

"What 'meteorological knowledge,'" I asked, "could the Acadian pioneers have possibly possessed?"

"A surprising amount," she answered. "They could tell you from experience exactly when to plant different crops." She smiled. "Don't think I believe if I step on a spider it will rain; I don't believe all their old adages. But they could forecast the weather with amazing accuracy."

Many of her collected folk ballads are sung unaccompanied. Early Acadians could rarely afford instruments to complement their singers anyway.

"So they used mouth music," she said.

"What's mouth music?"

"Like this." She demonstrated by hum-singing a tune through deliberately protruding lips and vibrating her forefinger rapidly up and down against the lips, from nose to chin, which sounded like a twanging instrument playing. Then for further illustration she played a cassette of a skillful farmer making mouth music.

Rural Acadians of the older generation are intensely loyal to tradition. One day, Charlotte Cormier remembers, the son of a well-known Acadian farmer and folk-singer returned home from Montreal, and, in a parlour chair, began to regale a family gathering with songs from his boyhood.

His listeners were horrified. No one had coaxed him. He was simply sitting there. He had forgotten all the important things.

"You just don't do that," an Acadian housewife told me. "It is very impolite."

Charlotte Cormier talks expressively, gesturing with her hands to emphasize a point. When she speaks of her Acadian identity as distinct from Quebec or France, her dark eyes flash.

Acadian folksongs are different from Quebec's, she points out, because many were brought direct from old France and others were written here in Acadia. The people had no contact with other French-speaking groups until about a century ago, so there is no exterior influence on their culture.

No more dramatic story exists in Canadian history than the emergence of the Acadians, who comprise 40 per cent of the population, into the mainstream of New Brunswick commercial, professional, and public life in the few short years since that time – a story so gradual and so quiet it is little known elsewhere. They had only one lawyer of their own, a few doctors and no dentists; now their university classes pour out graduates, they have risen to the top in politics, their choirs win national and world honours. As their own flag, they fly not the fleur-de-lis but the blue, white, and red flag of France with a golden star on the blue; their own special holiday is the Feast of the Assumption, August 15; their hymn "Ave Maris Stella," sung in Latin. New Brunswick, at this writing, is the only official bilingual province.

Born in Moncton, Charlotte Cormier was educated at Laval, Notre Dame d'Acadie in Moncton, the University of Indiana, and in France, where she attained her degree in ethnomusicology.

It was a timely moment, even a crucial moment, in Acadian cultural history when she began to mine old settlements for almost-forgotten lore. The last vestiges of an era were dying out – an era which great-grandparents recall with warmth in their eyes, when people were poor but happier than they knew, when they made their own entertainment at family parties, and the only music they heard was what they created themselves. Of an evening the wives would swap gossip in the parlour while the men sampled the host's home-brew in the kitchen. Later there would be singing and step-dancing and a pass-around of refreshments and, in their blissful ignorance of record-players and radio and movies and TV, everyone would go home thinking they had a great time.

Before the children were tucked in bed, a parent or grandparent might tell them once again the fairy-tale of Poor Jean, which was one of many Acadian equivalents to Goldilocks or Jack and the Beanstalk.

Jean lived with his mother in a hovel, and their sole earthly possession was a cow. Food became so scarce that one day the starving mother said, "Jean, you must sell the cow."

So Jean plodded toward town, and on the way he met the priest.

"I'll buy it for fifteen dollars," said the good father. "Here's the money, and put the cow in my barn."

Heading for the barn, Jean met the doctor, who said, "What have we got here?"

"We're so poor I had to sell the cow," the boy explained.

"I'll buy it for twenty dollars!" said the doctor. "Take the money, and leave the cow in my barn."

Jean pocketed the cash, but only a short distance onward he met the mayor.

"Well, well," said the dignitary. "What are we doing with a cow?"

"We are very hungry," said poor Jean. "We had to sell it."

"I'll take it off your hands," said the mayor. "Carry this fifteen dollars to your mother and put the cow in my barn."

Before he knew it, Jean was arrested. They told him he should get a lawyer.

"This is an easy case," the lawyer reassured him confidently. "All you have to do is act simple. Whenever anyone asks you for the money, just say, 'Di-di-diddlee-um, di-dee-di.' "

Throughout the trial, every time money was mentioned, the boy dutifully said, "Di-di-diddlee-um, di-dee-di."

Finally he got off, on the grounds of being simple-minded.

The grinning lawyer came to him and said, "How about my fee?"

Replied the boy:

"Di-di-diddlee-um, di-dee-dee."

The old story-teller's tales are fading away. Today most kids would rather spin the TV dial, and the pre-teens are more interested in discos, take-outs and drive-ins than the time-honoured ways of life.

Carefully Charlotte Cormier selected the Pre-d'en-Haut village area on the Petitcodiac for her research – not only because it's a very old parish, set in a nostalgic panorama with a huge white church and a backdrop of fragrant apple orchards, but also because it's off the beaten track.

"The people were extremely helpful," she said. "They really entered into the spirit of the project."

Some had never before seen the words of their favourite folk-songs written down. Neighbours phoned neighbours. Some remembered they had songs inscribed on the pages of faded old scribblers; a few produced songs penned in phonetic French, as they hadn't had much schooling until late in life. One home had no electricity yet; the housewife rummaged through old sheets of notes in the soft glow of oil lamps.

So Charlotte Cormier collected a wealth of material, taping amateur folk-singers in their homes far into the night, and making notes for archives, for Acadian folk-song books and for her singing recitals on the CBC network.

French as spoken in the Maritime provinces, several Memramcook residents reminded me, differs in many respects from Quebec French. Sometimes people from the two Canadian regions have a hard time understanding each other, or for that matter a Parisian visitor – much the same, I imagine, as when I go to a London theatre to see a play about Lancashire people; it takes me the first two acts even to grasp what they are talking about.

Quebecers often feel that their French is superior because the Acadians have intermixed so many English words into the language. But the Acadians in turn may feel superior because their language is essentially the genuine old French their ancestors brought over. In an isolated spot like Miscou island, off the northeast tip of New Brunswick, you may find a fisherman who speaks the same pure old French as the great comedy playwright Molière.

It's mainly in such remote areas that the word survivals of the 1600's are to be found in any substantial number. You may hear rural old folks talking about seventy and eighty and ninety not as *soixante-dix, quatre-vingt* and *quatre-vingt-dix* but as *septante, octante* and *nonante* – which seems to make streamlined sense even if it's obsolete.

Charlotte Cormier readily acknowledges she uses a lot of Acadian words in daily conversation – "we all do in New Brunswick."

I asked Mrs. Beatrice Boudreau of Memramcook, a helpful amateur historian, to cite offhand some of the most common differences between Quebec French and rural Acadian French. Here are her examples:

Window: In Quebec, *fenêtre*; in Acadia, *châssis*.
Fence: In Quebec, *clôture*; in Acadia, *bouchure*.
To come down (as in "to come down from Moncton to visit us"): In Quebec, *descendre*; in Acadia, *dévaler*.
To wound: In Quebec, *blesser*; in Acadia, *escloper*.
To give: In Quebec, *donner*; in Acadia, *bailler*.
To whistle: In Quebec, *siffler*; in Acadia, *subler*.
Twin: In Quebec, *jumeau*; in Acadia, *besson*.
Low-cut gown: In Quebec, *décolleté*; in Acadia, *décalvâtré*.
Rag: In Quebec, *guénille*; in Acadia, *brayon*.
To slow down: In Quebec, *ralentir*; in Acadia, *amodurer*.

Which Acadian word sounds strangest to Quebec ears?
"It's probably *dévaler*, for coming down for a visit," said Mrs. Boudreau with a laugh. "That always puzzles newcomers."

Age-old seasonal customs, too, are still perpetuated in rural Acadian hamlets. After the New Year is noisily welcomed by gatherings at midnight, the visiting around starts. Even great-grandmothers sit up alertly in their rockers, watching the front door in the hope that a tall dark-haired man will be the first to rap the knocker.

"That means good luck for the coming year," explained Mrs. Boudreau. "And then the children, of course, go around early on New Year's Day from door to door, wishing money for neighbours if they are poor, or good health if they are sick, and are given treats – a bagful of candy or doughnuts or a toy."

This was a big exciting event to youngsters a generation or two ago, for in numerous households of very humble means there were no Christmas "store gifts" as we know them today, only a sock containing an orange, an apple, some grapes, possibly a handful of mixed candy.

Here again we find a similarity between old Acadian and old English, Scottish, Irish, and Welsh customs in New Brunswick. Mrs. Linnea Calder, historian of the Roosevelt Campobello International Park on Passamaquoddy Bay, says the island is always a scene of lively activity after the New Year is ushered in. Young people vie with one another to race around and be the first to call at neighbours' homes and extend greetings and thus "bring them the luck" – and get treats of fruit or candy or silver coins in return.

Comments Mrs. Calder, a life-long resident: "Sometimes the children blow air into a paper bag and that's 'the luck.'

"Many householders have their own superstitions. One family may not want anybody but a blonde girl to be the first caller after midnight, another family insists on a dark-haired girl, or perhaps a dark-eyed boy.

"It's not unusual for parents to tell their own children, 'If you're out after midnight, don't come home till we've had a visitor.' If a member of the family is the first to enter, that's bad luck."

So it seems that in many ways the French-speaking people in Quebec and the Acadians are similar, only different; and the Acadians and the English are different, only similar.

When the World Came to an End

"Head for the hills!"

A strange cry to echo across the scraggly pine swamps and sandy flatlands of Florida – but echo it did in April of 1976.

And hundreds of followers of a religious cult, knowing that a calamitous tidal wave was about to engulf south Florida because their leaders had told them so, hastily packed their cars and trucks and drove for the hills of Tennessee, leaving behind their jobs and homes.

Nothing happened.

Outdoors editor Red Marston, writing later in *The St. Petersburg Times*, cautioned readers who felt like joking about the panic that they "should know something about a young British naval lieutenant named Saxby. Ever hear of the Saxby Gale? Know where the Bay of Fundy is?"

Then he narrated a phenomenon that had long interested him – the uncanny prophesy made in England in November, 1868, by Lieutenant S.M. Saxby, an instructor in naval engineering, that "a storm of unusual violence, attended by an extraordinary rise of tide," could scourge the earth early in the morning of October 5 the next year, a prophecy that came frighteningly true.

The Bay of Fundy, between New Brunswick and Nova Scotia, already had the highest rise and fall of tide in the world – fifty-three feet.

Under the driving force of screaming winds – a tempest

that had swept up the Atlantic shoreline from the Caribbean – Fundy's breakers overran the New Brunswick coast on the evening of October 4, inundating low-lying villages, while the gale wreaked devastation far inland throughout the night. Shipyard stocks crumpled, chimneys took off into the sky, church steeples vanished, houses were shorn of roofs, hundreds of boats were tossed up on shore, one farmer awoke to discover a schooner in his back yard, wharves were sluiced away, pedestrians were tossed about the streets, thousands of trees were uprooted, thousands of cattle and sheep and horses drowned, more than fifty people died, including crew members of the wrecked barque *Genie* at Lepreau, the Maine schooner *Rio* at St. Andrews, the schooner *Echo* at Grand Manan.

Expectably, amidst the fury of the storm, many people thought the end of the world was at hand and fell on their knees in prayer. In the loud silence afterward, scanning the debris, they stopped praying and started darkly suspecting that Lieutenant Saxby had been dabbling in witchcraft or, worse, was in league with the devil.

Was Lieutenant Saxby a sorcerer? Or a psychic? No, he was simply a scientist ahead of his time. He could reel off complicated meteorological and astronomical formulae without blinking. He had written in the London press nearly a year before that on the fateful date, October 4, "at 2 P.M. . . . lines drawn from the earth's centre would cut the sun and the moon in the same arc of right ascension. The sun's attraction and the moon's attraction will therefore be acting in the same direction. In other words, the new moon will be on the earth's equator when at the perigee and nothing more threatening can, I say, occur without a miracle."

The Saint John *Telegraph-Journal* on October 2 had republished the story of Lieutenant Saxby's warning from English papers, either as a serious alarm or a conversation novelty, whichever way people wanted to take it. Fortunately, many readers thought Lieutenant Saxby might be sane, and battened down their possessions and sheltered their livestock accordingly.

No weather spectacular like the Saxby Gale was experienced in the Maritime Provinces for more than a century – and then on February 2, 1976, in the wake of torrential rains, the "Groundhog Gale" struck.

Whether this disaster wielded any influence on the flight of the religious sect from Florida later that winter is not known – but in intensity and power the storm rivalled its famous predecessor. Both were borne by winds exceeding 100 miles an hour.

Once again roofs flew through the sky, ships were wrenched from their moorings, homes were flooded. At Cambridge Narrows a double-length covered bridge across the St. John River abruptly disappeared; the splintered matchwood was found far up-stream. On the deep frozen Kennebasis a young man fishing smelt through the ice was snatched up and hurled across the broad river, fatally injured. Paradoxically, a fishing boat landed on the highway and many cars landed in the water.

Because this storm came in the modern era, it had even more paralyzing impact than the Saxby Gale. Car windows were blown in; so were windows on tall buildings like Saint John's City Hall. People peering out saw through the lashing rain a scene that "looked like the end of the world" as big sheets of plywood sailed up and away like flying carpets, telephone poles and power poles sagged crazily in different directions, hanging on their wires. Families wrapped themselves in blankets as homes went heatless and lightless (and continued so for as long as five bitterly cold days afterward). Emergency centres were set up in churches and schools that had generators.

Through it all the Paramount Theatre marquee on tree-littered King Square kept cheerfully announcing its latest attraction – "Welcome To My Nightmare."

In this enlightened age, nobody blamed witchcraft; nobody blamed heaven; but many blamed the weather office, which had predicted south-southwesterly winds of thirty-five miles an hour with some precipitation.

Historically two other weather phenomena are still talked about. One is Cold Friday – February 8, 1861 – when the Saint John temperature suddenly plunged as far as thirty de-

below zero in the face of a rising gale, and thirty-six below at St. Andrews, thirty-eight below at Sackville. All travel was frozen. Dense vapour halted harbour ship movements. A train that left Saint John for Moncton had to come back – its wheels were spinning on icy tracks and the passengers were numb with cold.

The other is Dark Sunday – November 7, 1819 – when a mysterious gloomy haze over New Brunswick turned day into night, convincing countless people the end of the world might be near. Fears deepened when the darkness lasted not just for minutes, like an eclipse, but all morning and throughout a rainy afternoon. But next dawn the bright sun banished anxiety.

An additional phenomenon sometimes brought on noontime darkness in our Maritime great-grandfathers' day – but not since, and never again. This was the flight of multitudes of passenger pigeons, thunderously filling the sky for as long as three days. The size of the flocks was incredible: One seen in Kentucky in 1808 was estimated at two and a quarter *billion* birds. But hunters killed them mercilessly, blinding them with night lights in the tree branches and lashing them with staves, or hiding behind hillocks and knocking down the low-flying birds with poles. They sold them by the barrel to New York markets to retail at one cent apiece, or two cents for a good-sized seventeen-inch-long pigeon. Domestics signing work contracts specified they should not be served this fare more than once a week. But no more worry: the last passenger pigeon in the world died in 1914.

Curiously, although Maritimers like to recall hand-me-down tales of epochal storms, actually they live in a benign climate. Earthquakes, droughts, tornados, great extremes of heat and cold are practically unknown.

To find something really mind-boggling, you have to turn to non-weather disasters, including man-related ones.

The most catastrophic by far was the Halifax Explosion, a blast not surpassed in awesome magnitude by anything in known human history until the atomic bomb levelled Hiroshima.

Just consider – try to imagine – the unbelievable happenings that followed the baffling collision of the Norwegian "Belgian Relief" ship *Imo* and the munitions-laden French ship *Mont Blanc* in the half-mile-wide Narrows of Halifax harbour that fateful morning of November 6, 1917.

So tremendous was the detonation that part of Mont Blanc's anchor, weighing half a ton, was catapulted through the air for two and a half miles to land on the tip of Northwest Arm.

Its 1,200-pound gun soared in the other direction, travelling two miles before crashing into Albro Lake in Dartmouth.

The blast even bared the rocks of the harbour bed, sixty feet under the surface where the vanished *Mont Blanc* had been seen just a moment before.

Worsening the tragedy was the fact that the *Mont Blanc*, a floating time-bomb, had drifted for fifteen minutes while her deckload of highly volatile benzoil burned, the exploding drums sending up fascinating pillars of coloured flames into the sky.

This drew countless Halifax people to their windows to watch, unaware that in effect the benzoil was a fuse leading to the 4,000 tons of TNT and various chemicals in the holds.

Then came the terrific, ear-shattering blast – and in that shocking instant nearly 2,000 people died or were fatally hurt, and 9,000 injured. Showered with glass fragments speeding like bullets, 200 lost the sight of one or both eyes.

That meant one person in five in the city of 50,000 was a casualty.

And one in three left homeless – with a fierce blizzard just starting.

Some who weren't casualties had hair-raising experiences. Picked up by the vacuum of the explosion, several were wafted as far as half a mile away – and, to everyone's surprise, most alighted unhurt.

Inland from the waterfront, schools and churches and homes collapsed like cards, killing a few here, fifty there, 100 there, and nearly all 200 children in St. Joseph's Catholic School.

Other Canadian cities and New York and Boston sent hospital supplies and medical personnel – but for the immediate Halifax emergency little outside help was available.

Even afterward, unrelenting twenty-four-hour stints proved too much for some visiting doctors and nurses. It is told that a Moncton physician suffered a nervous breakdown, aggravated by the fact that near him stood a pail full of staring eyes – taken out without anaesthetics.

In this modern age, again, there was scant belief that the Almighty had smitten Halifax with this dreadful blow. Rather, and understandably, thousands of citizens thought at first that the port city was being bombarded by a German U-boat.

Eventually the court litigation reached the Privy Council Judicial Committee in England, which found both ships at fault because neither had observed the rules of the sea. But some older Haligonians aver to this day that the Kaiser somehow had a part in engineering the disaster.

As far as cost in lives is concerned, however, the chief anxiety of Nova Scotia over the years has been the spectre of sudden death – or lingering death – hovering over the men who go down deep into the colliery shafts to mine soft coal. Sometimes they travel deeper than any other miners in North America – even away out under the floor of the Atlantic. Many of the fatalities have resulted from "bumps," which are caused by excavated mines suddenly being compressed by Nature, trapping the men and shuddering the countryside above like an earthquake.

In Glace Bay, Sydney Mines, and Springhill the list of the lost has inexorably grown.

Springhill, for example, has been lamenting its sons ever since 1891, when Canada's worst mine explosion took the lives of 125 men and boys. Tragedy followed tragedy in recent decades – five miners in 1954; thirty-nine in 1956, and seventy-five in 1958, this disaster finally terminating Springhill's role as a leading coal producer.

Miraculous rescues of long-entombed miners have provided silver linings to brighten the grimness somewhat, but they do little to assuage the grief of stricken closely knit towns. Springhill, we must remember, had only 7,600 residents when the

1958 "bump" hit like an explosion. By the 1970's, after a steady emigration of youth westward, only 5,200 people remained.

Human nature being what it is, even a major mine disaster may be only a one-day wonder in the news – but ironically when fear, uncertainty, and tension surround a desperate rescue attempt, the whole world sits on the edge of its chair, even if only one or two lives are at stake.

In April, 1936, Moose River in Nova Scotia became a household name familiar to millions of North Americans. Housewives sat all day glued to their radios, listening to Frank Willis describing with barely repressed excitement the latest developments in the draegermen's efforts to save three men trapped 141 feet underground by a cave-in during inspection of a gold mine. One died, two were rescued alive after a dramatic race against rising flood waters and asphyxiation in what might have been their grave.

Of the same nature, if short-lived, was the agonizing experience of forty-one-year-old chimney expert Fred J. Esson at Saint John in the summer of 1954.

When he climbed up inside the 152-foot-tall brick smokestack of T. McAvity & Sons, the permanent iron ladder gave out under him only fifteen feet from the top – but he managed to claw and struggle up to sit exhausted astride the nine-inch-wide rim.

His ordeal was just beginning. Scorched by the sun, buffeted by the wind, nearly blinded by fly ash floating up from the chimney core, he clung to his perch for six hours while crowds gathered below and the locality became jammed with cars.

Most spectators just looked up silently, hands clasped, as the suspense grew almost unbearable. Enterprising food trucks were soon attracted to the scene like flies, vending sandwiches and coffee. A woman near me angrily cuffed her rambunctious youngster on the ear and warned him: "Keep watching the chimney or you won't see the man fall."

Finally, dramatically, a big Canso flying boat from Greenwood, N.S., lumbered into sight, circling the chimney summit and announcing over its amplifier: "Helicopter will be here in about three minutes."

And soon, like a determined dragonfly, a helicopter nosed around the chimney top to reconnoitre, then unreeled a thread-like cable with a metal basket dangling.

Came a breathtaking split-second when Fred Esson, half-blinded, reached out with one hand to grasp the basket in mid-air and somehow swung his feet and body into it.

A mighty spontaneous din arose from hundreds of car horns happily saluting the rescue.

Like Nova Scotia and Prince Edward Island, New Brunswick has reason to know that a fisherman's life is fraught with the threat of disaster. Rarely does a season go by without its tragedies, even in this day of ship-to-shore communication and other highly sophisticated equipment.

A visible reminder of old-time hazards is the Fishermen's Memorial at Escuminac on the northeast coast of the province, a tribute to the men who lost their lives when a sudden storm in June 1959 struck the flotilla which had gone out into Northumberland Strait to harvest the abundant run of salmon and mackerel.

The winds caught the forty-five boats unawares, because they had left home before the weather predictions were revised. Nearly half of them – twenty-two boats – foundered. Thirty-five fishermen drowned. And along the southern shore of Miramichi Bay, at Baie Ste. Anne, Bay du Vin, Hardwicke, Escuminac, homes went into mourning.

Of all New Brunswick's calamities, none compares in extent or in toll of life with the wild-rampaging Great Miramichi Fire of October 7, 1825.

It's appalling to look back on, even more than a century and a half afterward.

In the brief span of ten hours, one-fifth of the entire land area of the province was laid waste by flames.

It was a devastating blow to the great stands of towering white pines, which were so prized by the king's surveyors as masts for the Royal Navy. (Forty-four years later the Saxby Gale was to deal a death blow to the surviving pines.)

No one yet knows how many settlers, wives, and children died in the inferno – probably about two hundred.

Newborn babies were brought into a horrible world of roaring flames and dense choking smoke wherever the expectant mothers could find refuge, as in Strawberry Marsh or on Miramichi River rafts.

The river itself presented a strange spectacle of the companionship of fear – people standing up to their necks in water and, near them, cows and horses and deer and other animals of the forest doing the same.

It was impossible to outrun the onrushing wall of fire, for, on the momentum of its own draft, it was racing down from the Nor'West Miramichi at a mile-a-minute and leaping over all obstructions.

Some measure of the human tragedy can be sensed if you walk around in St. Paul's Church yard at Bushville. A monument honours the memory of Ann, wife of John Jackson, and her six children – all victims. The inscription:

> Forests were set on fire, and hour by hour,
>   They fell and faded and the crackling trunks
> Extinguished with a crash,
>   All earth was but one thought,
> And that was Death.

Those people who somehow came through it all felt they were hardly much better off. Many had no houses, no livestock, no provisions, and no hope of good timber to cut and export for another half-century.

Nearly 900 head of cattle had been crisped into embers in the Newcastle Parish area. Only about twelve of Newcastle town's 360 buildings remained intact, and six of seventy in Douglastown.

Little wonder that the dazed, char-blackened settlers, who had seen the skies open up and fire rain down, thought this was the hand of God. As a dirge-like Miramichi ballad recalled:

> Some said it was because the people's
>   Sins did rise to mountain high,
> Which did ascend up to Jehovah,

He would not see and justify.

In order to destroy their lumber
    And the country to distress,
He sent a fire in a whirlwind
    From the heaving wilderness.

And what a heart-rending panorama of desolation appeared the next day throughout the 8,000 square miles!

Ashes and live embers and smoking ground, chimneys standing stark and high out of stone cellars, streams still simmering, broiled salmon and trout floating on the surface, dead animals lying everywhere.

Sadly wrote Irish-born Miramichi historian Robert Cooney:

> A greater calamity than the Miramichi fire never befell any forest country, and has rarely been excelled in the annals of any other; and the general character was such that all it required, to complete a picture of the General Judgement, was the blast of a Trumpet, the voice of the Archangel, and the resurrection of the Dead.

Long gone now, of course, are all eyewitnesses of the Great Miramichi Fire. But here and there you still find older people who've talked with eyewitnesses.

John Leonard Mullin of Whitneyville, six miles from Red Bank, doesn't look it but he's so old he calls aging Paul Kingston, the white-thatched moosehorn blower of the Miramichi Folksong Festival, "Young Paul" to differentiate him from "Old Paul."

Actually he's pushing ninety-two, at this writing, but like many other Miramichiers Mr. Mullin is still robust and virile-looking with his black eyebrows and grey hair. He and his wife, two years his junior, have just celebrated their sixtieth wedding anniversary.

Though he's no longer working, he's unmistakably a Miramichi outdoorsman, with his plaid shirt and sweater, his heavy melton blue pants, belt and braces, thick socks.

"John Roy was in the J.D. Ritchie machine shop at the New-castle sawmill when I was a young fellow boating with the company – that is, towing logs from the booms and ferrying men off jams," recalled Mr. Mullin. "He was all through the fire – had to lay in the river at Newcastle and keep hauling wet blankets up over him; the water was lukewarm. The wind was blowing forty miles an hour. Embers were flying everywhere."

Himself, he had seen only burnt stumps, the last relics of the conflagration. "We used to make dug-out canoes out of pine – that is, what pine was left after the mast-cutting, the fire and the Saxby Gale."

His wife interjected, "A stone house, now a small museum, was the only building that withstood the Miramichi fire at Bartibog."

She added, of another place, "The fire cleaned everything right away except a Bible on top of a barrel. I've often heard my mother tell of it. People thought the fire was a judgement of God – Judgement Day."

Perhaps the most astonishing thing about the Great Saint John Fire of June 20, 1877, was that comparatively few people lost their lives – somewhere between eight and eighteen, most of them hit by falling buildings, compared with 200 fatalities in the Miramichi conflagration.

This was a near-miracle when you consider that in the short span of nine hours three-fifths of the city of 50,000 was destroyed, the South End being practically wiped out. More than 1,600 buildings were razed; 14,000 people were left homeless.

That is why today so many old sidewalk-hugging buildings bear a stone marker inscribed "1878" – they were erected in the year following the fire.

An odd commentary on the times: the holocaust levelled the City Hall, the Customs House, the Post Office, fourteen hotels, fourteen churches, eighty lawyers' offices, thirty-one tailor shops, ten blacksmith shops, five sail lofts, twenty-nine clothing stores, fifty-five boot and shoemakers' shops, among others – and 116 retail liquor shops and twenty-seven wholesale liquor establishments.

146

(In the last century the port city of Saint John had hundreds of taverns and liquor shops, even more than corner groceries. My mother often recalled her mother cautioning her, "Whenever you walk past a tavern, run." Said my mother, "I had to run almost all the way home.")

Historians of the day termed the cataclysm one of the worst fires in history, "more calamitous in its character than the great fires in Chicago and Boston."

In fact, it seems to have been the chronic fate of Saint John to be plagued by fires from its earliest days, even before it became Canada's first incorporated city in 1785.

Out-of-town visitors are always intrigued by the vivid old engravings on the walls of an upstairs lounge in the Union Club – fires, fires, and more fires, as if nothing else ever happened in the city. In the olden days this was partly true.

The first fire was in 1784, a year after the landing of the United Empire Loyalists – eleven houses fell to the flames.

In 1786 the city bought two fire engines from London – just in time for the outbreak in 1788 that destroyed General Benedict Arnold's store and threatened to spread.

Forty buildings burned on both sides of Prince William Street in 1823; the loss of £20,000 was regarded as enormous.

Then came the sweeping blaze of January, 1837, that demolished 115 buildings, including nearly all the commercial district. There had been a general prejudice against carrying insurance – which meant that many businessmen lost every penny.

In 1841 a winter fire took four lives; and in mid-summer Portland, in what is now the North End, saw sixty houses go up in flames.

So the melancholy chronicle went on: forty buildings lost in 1845, a destructive King Street fire in 1849, a Prince William Street fire in which seven people perished in March of 1877 – and then, in June, the Great Saint John Fire.

May 1899 brought the Indiantown Fire in the North End – more than 240 buildings gone, 300 families without shelter.

And on June 22, 1931, came the Great Dock Fire which on a summery afternoon obliterated many millions of dollars

147

worth of docks, sheds, grain facilities, ships. I was a night reporter at the time, and I saw a tall wisp of smoke on the West Side as I was driving out of the city with friends for a clambake. Three hours later, when we returned, the western side of the harbour was an uprolling wall of dense smoke. Fathers and mothers, dazed, were stumbling around looking for children, and children were wailing for parents. One smoke-smeared man was carrying the only possession he had saved – a huge framed colour-engraving of Mother Mary.

There were numerous other blazes since, but the one that haunts most people's memories was the Saint John jail fire of June 21, 1977, that snuffed out the lives of twenty-one inmates – a fire that hit only one small corner of the newly built, completely modern, fifteen-storey City Hall, yet killed more people than the Great Saint John Fire.

Many other blazes have seared New Brunswick – like the Fredericton fire of November 1830, which engulfed 300 houses, leaving 3,000 homeless . . . the St. Stephen fire of May 1877, which levelled eighty buildings and thirteen wharves, destroying thirty acres of the town . . . and the Great Campbellton Fire of July 1910, when wind-driven flames razed all but seven houses in the town, casting two thousand men, women and children into the streets – but, incredibly, without one fatality.

The runaway Great Saint John Fire, however, still burns most awesomely in the memory of people along the Bay of Fundy shore. There were so many examples of heroism as the wind-blown flames raged onward, often hurdling the firefighters, and "hissing and exploding everywhere," an eyewitness said.

Like the brave man who climbed up the outside of a three-storey burning home to pluck a sleeping infant from his crib, while the anguished mother watched from the square below.

And Postmaster Ellis, who stayed with the job till he got the last bag of mail aboard a boat . . . or the Western Union telegraph operator who put together a temporary office in Union Station to crackle out the news . . . or a man who refused to flee and kept dousing a hose of water on a building filled with volatile gas containers ... or a doctor who recruited a youth to help him pour buckets of water over kerosene stored on Reed's Point Wharf. ...

But there were bizarre, irrational incidents too –

One man ran out of his house with his arms full of kitchen utensils, leaving his good mahogany to burn.

Another householder was relieved to think he had saved an old tub and dipper – until he realized he had left all his personal papers to the flames.

A woman told her husband to be sure to carry out a bag – "It's got my family's century-old silver" – which he did, only to discover after the house burned that he had carried out the rag bag instead.

Pianos were hurled out third-storey windows to crash on the cobblestone streets.

Two sweating men carried worn-out carpets on their shoulders to safety.

From one home, every worthless article was salvaged in time – leaving a chestful of Continental dollars and the gun of Major Andre, Benedict Arnold's ill-fated emissary, to burn.

A man stood on the roof of the E.L. Jewett building, which was filled with heirlooms, sprinkling water out of a pitcher on each flying spark as it caught fire. Finally, as the flames got ahead of him, he was persuaded to descend, leaving the pitcher on a chimney ledge.

The house was completely destroyed – all but the gaunt chimney, and a lone pitcher standing on its ledge.

Some householders, mumbling about Judgement Day, were so paralyzed by shock they could only stand staring at the flames.

Not so the looters – but they were hardly more rational than anyone else.

One human jackal broke into a smouldering drug store and bore off a carton of "Unsurpassed Blood Mixture."

Another ran away with a case of "An Excellent Capillary Destroyer – Mrs. Allen's Zylobalsamum."

And another, hobbling along on a wooden leg, happily stuffed his pockets with Nonpareil Bunion and Corn Plasters.

The Man No Jail Could Hold

The High Sheriff and the Jailor marvelled at the demonstrations of Henry More Smith's versatile ingenuity – "the most astonishing genius and invention . . . perhaps in a manner and degree unequalled in the history of man" – despite the fact they both had indictments hanging over their sweating heads because of his escape.

It was only a little museum, as museums go – about three rooms downstairs in the Centennial Building in the village of Hampton – but the enthusiastic white-haired curator was as proud of the place as if it were the Smithsonian Institution itself.

And deservedly so, for W. Harvey Dalling's Kings County Historical Society Museum is a fascinating repository of local mementos from the last two centuries – an example of the usefulness of regional museums as adjuncts to the large New Brunswick Museum in Saint John, the first in Canada.

"We have 2,162 articles here," Mr. Dalling, a retired teacher, was saying, "mostly from United Empire Loyalist days. I'm surprised at how many people are interested."

Here we found upwards of a hundred photos of the colourful steamboats that plied the St. John River and its tributaries for nearly a century and a half. And antique typewriters, beds, quilts, dinner plates, looms, cumbersome keys, a set of 1854 standard brass weights and measures, a century-old collapsable highchair on wheels which converts into a stroller, seven ponderous clocks, one with a level inset in the bottom and a thermometer in the top.

To me there were two unforgettable exhibits. One was a display of quaint-looking skates, with wooden tops and very long steel blades curled up in a twirl in front like Walt Disney pixie shoes, complete with screws for fastening the tops to your boot heels, and straps for harnessing the tops around your insteps and toes. To save weight, the long blades were punched with a series of holes.

"These Long Reach speed skates, called 'reachers,' were the pioneers of all modern speed skates having a prolonged heel," Mr. Dalling explained. "Made by J.A. Whelpley at his factory at Greenwich on the St. John River about 1870. You see, being low-down, these skates were less likely to cramp the ankle, and so were peculiarly adapted to long journeys, hundred-mile trips being a frequent occurrence on the river in those days."

History was made by the Whelpley skates not only because they introduced a revolutionary new design, but because on these unorthodox flashing "reachers" in the 1880's Hugh McCormick, a farm lad from the Willows on the Kennebecasis River, astounded the sports fraternity by winning one speed-skating meet after another in Canada and the United States until climactically he captured the world championship. Astounding, too, was the fact that he was dethroned in 1893 at the classic old Victoria Rink in Saint John by Fred Breen, who grew up on the Kennebecasis only a half-hour's skate from the Willows. And so two world titlists and their skates all came from Kings County.

This was a generation before the second great New Brunswick speed-skating era in Saint John which produced the phenomenal Charles I. Gorman, the "world's fastest human," "the human dynamo," "the man with the million-dollar legs." Wounded twice in the right leg at Arras in the Great War, he exercised unceasingly to strengthen the muscles, managed to return to speed-skating in 1921 and five years later won the world championship. Next year he shattered half a dozen world records. New Brunswickers confidently claim he was the fastest competitive skater who ever lived.

And then you notice in a modest showcase a well-worn pair of handcuffs, with a big iron key, and leg shackles – relics of the most mysterious man who enlivened the long history of this part of Canada.

These restraints had held Henry More Smith in 1814 – but, like everything else High Sheriff Walter Bates and Jailor William Dibblee resorted to in desperation, even thick iron collar-clamps and ox-chains, they didn't hold him for long.

"You probably noticed next door we have the old jail from Kingston, across the Kennebecasis about fifteen miles from here," Mr. Dalling said, and I remembered the grim building we had passed, made of huge granite blocks, with heavily barred windows. "But that wasn't Henry More Smith's jail; his was an even older one, under the original courthouse at Kingston. The Macdonald School occupies part of the site today."

I couldn't help thinking the "newer" Kingston jail would be old by some more recent communities' standards. Built probably in the 1830's, it was moved to Hampton in 1870 when Kingston was shorn of its status as Kings County shiretown, and was used for prisoners for a century. Lately there have been reports it will be reactivated as a jail.

What a herculean task the moving job must have been! Stone block by stone block, the two-storey building was dismantled, then hauled across the Kennebecasis ice in winter by teams of oxen, to be reassembled at Hampton. (You can imagine what would happen in the twentieth century: first the authorities would suggest it would be cheaper to build anew than transfer the old building; then, if pressed by historical societies, they would estimate $225,000 for the removal job to be done by multiple tractors; the bill would finally turn out to be $535,000, after which there would be a Royal Commission of enquiry, whose findings, costing $275,000, would be shelved, prompting intermittent Opposition complaints for three years afterward.)

Mr. Dalling proved to be a mine of information about Henry More Smith, because he was familiar with the written recollections of Sheriff Bates and other contemporaries, also of Fred M. Sproule who in 1913, addressing the Hampton high-school students, took them back a century to the adventures of the great deceiver.

Reminisced Mr. Sproule, "Reverend Elias Scovil, rector of Kingston, was very attentive to the physical as well as spiritual wants of the prisoner. I have derived much of my information from the respected wife of this reverend gentleman. In my schoolboy days at Kingston, the remarkably well-preserved old lady would often delight me by giving me details of this and other interesting events. . . . "

It all began because of a skittish horse.

If the horse hadn't bucked and shied so nervously, the Kingston jail would never have heard of Henry More Smith, a prisoner destined to attract attention all over the world.

The young man, apparently an English immigrant, had managed to get out of Nova Scotia, where he worked as a pious and exemplary-mannered farmhand, married his employer's daughter, robbed people right and left. His cunning barefaced style was already apparent. For example, three Admiralty volumes vanished from the Halifax office of the chief justice, who offered a no-questions-asked reward. Smith promptly returned the books, blandly said he bought them from a stranger, and collected the three guineas. As a tailor he measured a Windsor young man for a new coat and brought it on the specified date – and then the buyer was arrested in Halifax on behalf of an angry sputtering gentleman who said it had been stolen from him.

Smith arrived in New Brunswick on horseback, a peddler selling watches and other wares, taking lodgings outside Saint John.

He soon offered a deal hard to turn down. Colonel Daniel of the 99th Regiment needed a handsome black horse to make a matched team.

"I know of an excellent match for your horse for £50 in Cumberland," confided Smith. "If you will advance me £15, I will leave my own horse in security and take a bay sloop to Nova Scotia and bring the animal back."

This was child's-play: Smith would simply steal a mare

from a pasture he'd noticed outside the city, ride it to Cumberland, sell it, steal the black horse and ride it back to claim the full amount.

But the mare kept rearing up and dodging out of his reach, and Smith had to set forth on foot – weighed down by a military saddle and bridle he purloined from an army friend. That night he reached Norton, stole a black horse, but soon felt so exhausted he had to sleep – and slept too long.

Espied leaving a barn next day, he was finally overtaken at Pictou, N.S., by the irate horse owner, F.W. Knox, and arrested and sent back to Kingston.

Now began an historic confrontation – Smith vs. The Law – that was to go on for many months.

No one could have pled innocence more persuasively. Smith earnestly told the judges he had bought a horse for £10, then exchanged it, plus £15, with a stranger for the Knox horse – even producing a full receipt signed by "James Churman."

No one believed him for a moment.

Before he could be brought to trial, Smith fell violently sick. Afflicted with coughing, a sharp pain in his side, raising blood and evacuating blood, he declined visibly until finally all realized the end was near. Every visit of his physician only emphasized it anew. He even made his will, leaving his money, £3, to jailor William Dibblee (when Dibblee considerately offered to look after it for him, Smith gasped it would be all right where it was, in his bunk).

The violent death throes continued, night after night, wearing down the nervous systems of the good people of Kingston, conscious as they were of the fact this would be the first hanging for horse-stealing in New Brunswick, and imbued with sympathy for the abject Englishman dying friendless in the New World.

Finally came the long-awaited climax. In apparent agony Smith complained faintly that his feet had frozen up to his knees and begged John Dibblee, the jailor's son, to fetch a heated brick, which the young man did, leaving the cell door open. Meanwhile Mrs. Scovil, the good rector's wife, had sent her black servant Amy with a feather bed for the poor miscreant to die on.

What transpired next might have been comic if it did not have such grave overtones.

When John Dibblee sprinted back to the expiring man with the hot brick, he was dumbfounded to find the cell empty: Smith had vanished, along with his clothes and boots – not forgetting the £3 he intended to bequeath to the jailor.

Obviously he must have passed by the open door of a room where the rector and the jailor were sitting talking about funeral plans.

At this juncture Amy plodded in with the feather bed – and was shooed away by the exasperated officials.

Dutifully she returned home with the report, "Massa say Smith gone and don't need bed."

Weeping, Mrs. Scovil replied, "Poor man, so he is dead. Well, Amy, run and carry this winding sheet to lay Smith out in."

When Amy arrived at the jail, the rector himself confronted her and said with a sigh, "You may take these back. Smith is gone."

When she innocently enquired where Smith had gone, the good clergyman shrugged:

"I don't know, unless the devil has taken him."

The news spread like a forest fire – "Smith is gone!" – and naturally everyone assumed he was now with his Maker.

Several privately waxed angry at Mr. Knox, the horse-owner who had him arrested, for Smith had blamed his feebleness on a pistol-whipping by Mr. Knox in Pictou – one blow "felled me to the ground like a dead man" – and he had a swollen and discoloured bruise on his side to prove it.

When a messenger notified High Sheriff Bates, he said sorrowfully, "Ah, poor fellow, I expected it. What time did he die?"

"But he's gone – gone clear off."

"Impossible!" the high sheriff retorted. "He can't be far from his sick bed."

To add to the general consternation, W.H. Lyon went to visit the Scribner household that evening and confirmed the report that Henry More Smith was dead – "I know, because at dusk tonight on the way here I saw Smith's ghost pass me by only a short distance away, without touching the ground."

Now not only Smith was in trouble.

Wrote Fred M. Sproule:

"Much discussion took place concerning the escape, and some even went so far as to say that it had been carried out by the officials. Both the sheriff and jailor were Freemasons, and it was alleged (though without any atom of proof), that Smith was one. For some time there had been a great agitation against Freemasonry and this was gladly taken as an additional ground for condemnation. Fortunately, this prejudice has been very largely removed from the public mind and a better opinion exists as to the benefits of this world-wide brotherhood. When the court convened at which Smith was to be tried, the grand jury found true bills against the sheriff and jailor for the escape. These were, however, later dropped."

What happened thereafter was to recur frequently whenever Smith escaped: because he was so resourceful, the authorities always supposed next day he must be far away – perhaps he had covered a hundred miles by changing horses.

In reality he was probably just a few miles up the road, breakfasting in a hospitable farm family's kitchen – and planning to appropriate the clocks and mantel ornaments when he bade them goodbye.

These he would sell as a peddler at his next place of call, while pilfering that home's watches and jewellery and silverware.

You would hardly call his attitude happy-go-lucky; it was more devil-may-care, as if he could talk himself out of any emergency, or if not, he could break out. For sheer bare-faced gall, the god-fearing Loyalist households had never imagined anything like it.

After entering the home of a Mr. Bailes on the road to Gagetown, breaking into a trunk and making off with a silver watch, eight dollars, a pocketbook and a new pair of velvet pantaloons, he was pursued by a posse armed with a description that Bailes furnished of the man who had slept in front of his barn door.

Next morning Henry More Smith, purporting to be a Frenchman on his way to Fredericton on business, accompanied by an Indian paddler, stopped at Vail's Tavern on Grimross Neck for breakfast. At the same moment, oblivious of everything around him, Mr. Bailes was having breakfast at Vail's and busily writing out advertisements to catch the thief. The fugitive enjoyed a leisurely meal and left unnoticed – taking along a set of silver teaspoons from a dining-room closet.

Meanwhile, with Judge Chipman presiding, the court formally convened in Kingston to try the alleged horse-thief. Even the New Brunswick attorney-general was present – but the defendant wasn't.

Day by day the court hopefully reconvened, but the only new development came in mid-afternoon on the third day, when Mr. Knox's servant in great agitation sought out the complainant in the courtroom and told him, "Sir, your other horse is gone now too."

Almost apoplectic, Mr. Knox raged loudly that his life was in peril as long as Smith was at large, for a strange Indian had been seen near his pasture, and His Honour concurred that there had been serious derelictions of duty. So the reward notice of $40 for Smith's capture (which can be still seen in the aging files of the Saint John newspapers in the Regional Library) was doubled. Later it was to be escalated again and again.

In his wanderings, the fugitive assumed varied roles, even telling one suspicious group that his name was Bond, that he was on the trail of the infamous jailbreaker from Kingston, whom he was anxious to bring to justice – "the scoundrel certainly should be hanged."

Whenever he travelled, Smith kept collecting useful or saleable goods, even an armful of freshly laundered linens.

Anyone might think he would hesitate to rob such a powerful figure as the attorney-general, who was entertaining at his residence in Fredericton. But Smith didn't disdain the top official of the law; he cleared his hall racks of five overcoats, three cloaks, numerous tippets and comforters.

When finally caught and arrested near Fredericton, the escapee was taken back to Kingston aboard a sloop – wearing handcuffs and an iron collar fashioned from a flat bar an inch and a half wide, hinged with a clasp secured by a padlock. A ten-foot iron chain, extending from the collar, was held by a hired watchman.

In the light of later events, we know that Henry More Smith could easily have freed himself from these bonds if he wanted to; but he seemed to have a strange compulsion not only to steal but to test his cunning intermittently against whatever manacles and fetters the forces of the law could devise.

Confidently the following morning High Sheriff Bates and Jailor Dibblee inspected the jail. First they inspected Smith himself, minutely, even to the hairs of his head, for he had an unbelievable knack of secreting escape implements. The prison – twenty-two by sixteen feet – had three stone and lime walls three feet thick; one side was a partition from the debtor's jailroom. Even the partition of timber was a foot thick, lathed and plastered. The door was of two-inch plank, doubled and lined with sheet iron, with three iron bar hinges. In fact, the whole place was simply impregnable: "the best jail in New Brunswick," officials always said.

Extremely wary now, the officials fastened on Smith's right leg a chain "no more than long enough to allow him to reach the necessary [the toilet], and to take his provision at the wicket door. The end of the chain was fastened to the timber of the floor by a strong staple . . . so he could not reach the grated window by five or six feet."

Everything, in short, was perfect.

It wasn't.

Night after night, when strange noises were heard from Smith's cell, they investigated to find him almost free again, on the brink of escape.

He broke iron chains as if they were daisy chains. He bent and snapped iron neck bars made by a blacksmith. He drew staples out of the floor. No matter how often they searched him and his cell – even probing down "the necessary," just in case – he somehow artfully concealed knives and improvised fine saws from such things as watch springs. They kept adding to and tightening his restraints until he was wearing forty-six pounds of iron, and could only sit or lie on the floor.

Often, when found out, he obligingly showed his captors how he contrived his bids for liberty.

There were times, the high sheriff admitted, when he felt misgivings. Could it be possible that they were actually persecuting a more or less guiltless man? After all, the prisoner did have contusions where he said Mr. Knox hit him with the pistol.

And he had insisted so vociferously on his innocence that he had even spurned an invitation from Lieutenant Baxter to join the New Brunswick Regiment and thus escape from confinement – and the hangman's noose.

As for that transparent excuse that he bought the Knox horse from a "Mr. Churman," High Sheriff Bates had occasion the next day to drive to Saint John, twenty miles distant, with Dr. Adino Paddock, Sr. While they were tying up their horses at Nathaniel Golding's tavern in Hampton, "we perceived a man mounting a horse in great haste, who immediately rode off with all possible speed, as though he were in fear of being overtaken." Mrs. Golding replied to their suspicious enquiries, "Oh, he's a stranger who's been in two or three times lately. His name is Chuman or Churman." The news of this elated the prisoner in Kingston, but no further trace of the man was ever found.

Through the winter, as his trial approached, Smith seemingly became obsessed, attempting to hang himself or starve to death, yelling and screaming and hallooing, quoting Scripture, threatening to burn down the building, but speaking directly to no one. He was, they said, undoubtedly mad.

In May 1815, still unspeaking, acting like an idiot, he was tried for horse-stealing at long last.

He fought the constables so strenuously he smashed all wooden railings of the prisoner's box with his feet, and he had to face the proceedings with his arms bound by rope anchored in one direction while his tied feet were facing the opposite direction. Found guilty – even though the jury found him "mute from visitation of God" – Smith heard the sentence: "Death, without the benefit of clergy." So the convicted man was returned to his harsh fetters and frigid cell and was placed on death rations: one pound of bread a day, with water.

Then began such a wondrous exposition of Smith's talents that interest was excited throughout North America and Europe.

High Sheriff Bates wrote letter after letter about it, ecstatically and at great length, to the attorney-general, the Honourable Thomas Wetmore. From bedding straw and scraps of clothing and his own blood Smith had fashioned an entire set of miniature characters who played music and danced as the creator sang or whistled a tune. He was adding new characters daily. Already several visitors, including a Scotsman, a Pennsylvania doctor, an Irish doctor, and a Bostonian, had acclaimed the performance as excelling anything they had seen in the world.

Mr. Sproule, who spoke to the Kingston school a century later, was skeptical about the whole thing. He asserted: "He scraped the outlines of other figures on the plaster of his cell which I have myself seen. I have heard it very confidently asserted by the oldest resident of Kingston that these figures moved in concert with his happy family. This being manifestly impossible, I have often thought that Smith must have been a powerful hypnotist or mesmerist, who was able to make people see things just as he wanted.

"I have always accepted, with a great degree of allowance, these fabulous stories of Smith's exploits and if you will stop to consider that at the time he was alleged to be performing these wonderful feats, there were indictments hanging over the heads of the sheriff and jailor for the escape, it might easily be seen that if the public were led to believe in his supernatural powers, it would be easy to meet the charges. This actually transpired and the prosecution dropped as I have before noted."

Such cynics – if there were any in 1815 – did not deter High Sheriff Bates from describing Smith's performances as "the most astonishing genius and invention: perhaps in a manner and degree unequalled in the history of man."

It's odd to think that if the old court records are available somewhere, Smith is probably listed only as "horse-thief."

In actuality he was an early-day Houdini, a super-confidence man, magician, mystic, will-o'-the wisp, bilingual fraud, preacher and religious hypocrite, prophet, mind-reader, fire-maker, master tailor, puppeteer, mesmerist, contortionist, natural-born engineer – and, of course, a very likeable horse-thief.

A prophet? Yes, he told the high sheriff many things of which he could not possibly have possessed foreknowledge – including looking in his teacup to foretell that "three important papers, including a large one about me" will arrive by four o'clock. Sure enough, they did: two letters – and a bigger missive containing his pardon!

Ironically High Sheriff Bates had a hard time persuading Smith to leave his cell. First he brought a tailor to make a coat, but Smith, who prided himself in this skill, said, "Let me look at your hands and fingers. You are no tailor, you look more like a blacksmith – you shall never make a coat for me." Whereupon Smith made his own beautiful coat and waistcoat, with only a candle's illumination for a few minutes in the darkness.

Fire-maker? Yes, he had never needed to freeze, he admitted. He could "make fire anytime in one hour" – and he proved it by igniting chips in his cell.

With heartfelt relief High Sheriff Bates took him to Saint John, put him aboard a sloop for Windsor, Nova Scotia, his old home – and stayed to make sure the sails disappeared over the horizon.

(That, apparently, was a favourite riddance device in the old days. A few years earlier Colonel David Fanning, a boastful Loyalist guerrilla leader in the U.S. Revolutionary War, detested by his upright fellow Loyalists in Saint John, was haled before the court on a trumped-up accusation that he had raped a young black girl. The judge sentenced this Kings County member of the New Brunswick Legislative Assembly to be hanged, but offered to commute the sentence if Fanning would leave New Brunswick for good. He gladly went to Digby, N.S.)

Incidentally, Smith demonstrated his powers as a mind-reader in Nova Scotia. When he stopped at a hostel for breakfast and went out to wash, a suspicious maid opened his bundle, which was found to contain fifteen watches and many other valuable items. "He must have stolen them!" Then she tied up the bundle and left it looking exactly the same. When Smith reappeared, he asked her, "There were just fifteen watches, were there?" Taken aback, she was surprised into saying, "Yes." He added, "But you were mistaken about my stealing them. I came by them honestly."

To everyone's surprise, Smith evidently ignored his wife in Nova Scotia and travelled on to the United States and later central Canada, his career following the usual spectacular course – brazen thefts, arrests, astounding break-outs, recaptures, failing health, blood brought up, public sympathy.

In the Southern states he renamed himself "Reverend Henry Hopkins," preached to the multitudes, and was amazed himself by how many devoted back-sliders followed him to hear still further inspiring sermons on the Word.

It was always easy for Sheriff Bates to follow Henry More Smith's trail, even though his former prisoner kept changing his name, his outward appearance, and his nationality. The clue was that his minor crimes reported in the press were invariably in keeping with his imaginative nature.

One day *The Boston Bulletin* related, under the heading "BEWARE OF PICKPOCKETS!":

As the stage coach, full of passengers, was on its way to this city a few evenings since, one of the passengers rang the bell, and cried out to the driver to stop his horses, as his pockets had been picked of a large sum of money since he entered the coach; and at the same time requested the driver would not let any of the passengers get out of the coach, it being dark, until he, the aforesaid passenger, should bring a light in order to have a general search. This caused a general feeling of pockets among the passengers, when another passenger cried out that his pocketbook had also been stolen. The driver did as directed until the gentleman who first spoke should have time to have procured a lamp, but whether he found it or not remained quite uncertain. But no doubt he found the light he intended should answer his purpose, as he did not make his appearance in any other light. However, the passenger who really lost his pocketbook, although it did not contain but a small amount of money, thinks he shall hereafter understand what is meant when a man in a stage coach calls out thief, and that he will prefer darkness rather than light, if ever such an evil joke is offered to be played with him again.

You can imagine Sheriff Bates in Hampton reading this, with an insight no Bostonian could possess.

"Well, here we go again," he would say with a resigned but almost amused shrug. And he'd remind his wife to have his travel bag ready in case the Americans apprehended the fugitive, because he would like to see Smith again and talk with his jailors – as he was to do several times in later years.

Sheriff Bates grudgingly liked and admired the man. So did Fred Sproule, a century later.

After all, Smith made a lot of trouble, but he never caused violence or pain to anyone but himself.

Today, nearly two centuries later, the famous prisoner is anything but dead in the old village of Kingston.

When the annual Kingston Loyalist Days parade is held, you may see a caged Henry More Smith travelling in an historical float.

A panic was precipitated in the Kingston School a few years ago when a rumpled, slept-in bed was discovered in the office. "Henry More Smith is back!" went the cry around the classrooms. (A teacher, marking exams late, had stayed overnight.)

A farmer owned a steer that was forever knocking down the pasture fence and escaping. Naturally he named the animal "Henry More Smith."

And it would be hard to count how many head-strong tomcats and dogs on the peninsula answer to the same name.

Comments Mrs. John Calder, a Kingston Peninsula historian, "Everybody here knows the old story, and everyone would gladly contribute old things to a Henry More Smith Museum if it were set up some day."

Pupils of the aging Macdonald Consolidated School a generation ago could see, in the basement, the archways of the old jail cells. Since then the basement has been "improved," and all you can see now are bricked-in arches painted over.

Eventually, in the continuing expansion of the school, the original cells should be restored and a unique local museum established. It would be really authentic, not a hoked-up plastic replica – a very special tourist attraction of a type no other place in North America could match.

These Mysteries Still Cry Out for Answers

What strange "unknown mysterious power" was possessed by Henry More Smith in the preceding chapter? Was it supernatural? Was it black magic? Was he, as some superstitious villagers thought, in cahoots with Old Nick?

Or did he just have an extraordinary ability to shrink his arm and leg muscles at will and contort his body – as well as possessing a born mechanical genius for outwitting anything a locksmith could devise, including iron bars and chains that would hold an ox?

Even if some plausible explanation for these questions may be offered, how can anyone dismiss the eerie fact that visitors peering into his cell saw a doll orchestra playing while other miniature characters danced around gracefully? This suggests mass hypnotism.

Perhaps any clever person with a gift for acting might feign a decline to death's threshold as Henry More Smith did so convincingly. But how can skeptics shrug off the startling point that this prisoner was kept in a stone jail, without heat of any kind, through an icy New Brunswick winter (when temperatures drop to thirty degrees below zero Fahrenheit) – and yet whenever officials looked in on him, *he was comfortably warm and, in fact, his shackles were warm too?*

What gave the Saint John-built clipper-type windjammer *Marco Polo* such dazzling speed that she was bannered in Liverpool, England, "The Fastest Ship in The World"? (She even beat a steam packet on the immigrant run to Australia.) Was it her unconventional design? Or was it the "hog" (twist) in her hull that resulted from the abortive launching in 1851?

What kind of motive power propelled Canada's first automobile, a three-wheeled contraption that appeared on the streets of Saint John, N.B., in 1851?

Brain-child of Thomas Turnbull, an ingenious carpenter and tinkerer, the horseless carriage had three wheels – one in front for "guiding," two in the rear that drove the vehicle – frontwards and backwards at speeds up to 30 m.p.h. The operator worked big levers and seemed to have marvelous control.

But the inner mechanism was concealed within wooden sheathing, and Turnbull said he would reveal nothing until the invention was patented. He never did disclose the secret – and today historians are still wondering whether the engine used steam, oil or some early form of electrical power.

How foresighted were the newspaper editors of that era! One, ignoring completely the great potential of this carriage for people everywhere, suggested it would make an entertaining device for New Brunswick to send to the forthcoming Great Exhibition in London, England, and try to get ahead of Nova Scotia for once.

Another editor, labouring under the impression that working the levers was what made the carriage go – like a child's pedal car of today – offered the inspired idea that if one man at the levers could operate the carriage with a passenger sitting beside him, why couldn't two men busily working levers make a bigger carriage go with ten or twelve passengers?

"Every Man His Own Horse" was the enthusiastic heading of the article. The editor went on to say what a wonderful boon this carriage should be to people who travel around a lot – "particularly the physicians, who are subject to so much circumlocomotion as they make their daily rounds of house calls."

House calls? That *was* a long time ago.

Who were the first Western explorers of the Bay of Fundy coastline?

Controversy has swirled around the subject for generations, but every now and then a glimmer of new light is shed. Discovery of ancient settlement sites in Newfoundland and far inland in North America has pretty well confirmed that the Norsemen were on the Atlantic coast centuries before Columbus set sail.

Some researchers point out close similarities between Viking sagas about Odin, fearsome but gentlemanly king of the gods and nemesis of evil giants in Norse mythology, and Indian tales about Glooscap, the man-god of the Micmacs and Maliseets, who was all-powerful, sometimes belligerent but often benevolent, with an eye to the humorous side of life. And Lokker, the Norse satan, closely resembles Lox of the Indians. In these historians' minds the only question is who borrowed folklore from whom.

Every province and state stands up for its own claims. In New Brunswick a widely held belief is that the Vinland of the Norse explorers around 1,000 A.D. was the mouth of the Miramichi River. Many think that the ancient Straumey described by the Norsemen included Grand Manan Island and Deer Island with its eddies and world's biggest tidal whirlpool.

Champlain and de Monts deservedly received acclaim for their early exploring, chronicling, and chart-making; but they realized others had been there before them. At the outlet of the St. John River in 1604, they reportedly found the Indian chief to be shrewd and experienced in bartering with Europeans. On a later voyage they discovered at the head of the bay an ancient cross almost rotted away. French, Basque, and Portuguese fisherman had ranged the bay in the 1500's and probably before. One of the first to explore it may have been Joam Alverez Fagundas, to whom King Emmanuel of Portugal around 1521 granted title to whatever lands he chanced upon beyond the seas.

The name "Fundy" was believed for years to be derived from the Portuguese "fondo" ("deep"); but historian Dr. W.F. Ganong later asserted "Fundy" was an English corruption of the French word "fendu," or "split," which on early Bay of Fundy charts referred to Cape Split at the Minas Basin entrance. De Monts re-christened it "La Baie Françoise," but the new name didn't stick.

There are almost as many theories as historians. Brooklyn scholar and archaeologist Frederick J. Phol insisted that the Maritime Indians' hero-god Glooscap was none other than Henry Sinclair, Prince of Orkney and ruler of the Shetland Islands, who with 200 soldiers was thought to have antedated Columbus in the New World by braving out the cold winter of 1398 amidst the Micmacs near Pictou, N.S. The imaginative natives supposedly attributed to the white stranger-god great powers that became magnified as the tales were passed down through generations.

Phol followed the trails of the Micmac tribe's annual migrations along Northumberland Strait and the Bay of Fundy shore, seeking proof of his theory. But most of the distant past continued to be locked in obscurity. He did determine some similarities, possibly significant, such as the fact that Glooscap and the Prince both had three daughters, both knew the uses of iron, both possessed intoxicating liquors.

Such research may be essentially a task for professional scientists, but there are ways in which everyday citizens can help. They're not too likely to find any traces of wrecked ships left behind by those European fishermen who apparently reaped rich harvests in the Bay of Fundy in the 1400's and 1500's (and, like today's sports anglers, discreetly made no public mention of their favourite spots).

One way, however, is to report any finding of what could be early explorers' markings – for instance, the signatures known to have been carved in stone by Captain Bartholomew Gosnold at several locations along the New England coast in 1602.

It was this high-born Suffolk Englishman who named Cape Cod, later ventured up the coast of Maine and possibly the Bay of Fundy, and on a subsequent voyage helped found the colony of Virginia.

From time to time it has been reported that one of these "Gosnold inscriptions" was discovered on the rocky New

Brunswick shore – but researchers regret this has not yet been confirmed, for it would introduce an entirely new element in our regional history.

Is there buried treasure still to be found in New Brunswick? Did swaggering buccaneers of the Spanish Main really conceal loot somewhere in the uncounted coves of the Bay of Fundy?

Public attention for years has been focussed on the Nova Scotia searches – the interminable attempts to penetrate the intricately contrived platform barriers in the Oak Island excavations, and the successful underwater quest for gold coins and other valuables in the wreck of a payship off Cape Breton.

But with less fanfare, persistent treasure diggers in New Brunswick have got away with rich finds – not pirate gold, usually, but often money hidden by sea captains or by fleeing Acadians in the mid-1700's.

Caleb Stokes of Salem, Massachusetts, retrieved from Belleisle Bay in 1883 an iron chest of gold, worth $13,000, lowered there decades before by a British privateer. A St. Martins man got $8,000 worth of coins in a small iron box washed out near the West Quaco Creek. In the Fort Beausejour area a farmer excavating a cellar found more than $30,000 in gold; he moved away immediately to the United States.

That's the trouble. People who came upon sudden wealth clammed up. Next thing you knew, they had packed up and moved away. No one knows for sure, as an example, whether famed Marysville lumber baron Alexander (Boss) Gibson, really got his start in the last century by sending divers down into the waters off Dipper Harbour to recover Spanish gold dollars and silver coins from the wreck of the War of 1812 payship H.M.S. *Plumper*. It was right after this that close-mouthed Gibson began buying up vast timber reserves, the foundation on which his industrial empire was built.

Many fool's-gold chases developed, too. On the shore of Red Head, a promontory just outside Saint John, people excitedly reported finding old gold coins. This caused a treasure-hunting boom.

Not until later was it learned that in the early 1800's British sailors were paid in gold but had nowhere to spend it. The navy wouldn't let them patronize the innumerable bars and houses of pleasure in the Port of Saint John. Result: for something to do, the deck hands bounced gold pieces off the rocks of Red Head in the old coin-matching game – and inevitably an occasional coin got lost in the crevices.

I realized there was still gold to be found in the Fundy islands when I stood beside Galen Sheehan, assistant manager of Roosevelt Campobello International Park, as we cruised on a fishing boat around the entire island, a three-hour trip. I had just ordered a dozen jars of pickled herring to bring home with me.

On the inhospitable northeast side of Campobello (a New Brunswick island off the coast of Lubec, Maine), there were high cliffs, cliffs, and more cliffs, with straggly trees, vines and daisies valiantly clinging to the steep slopes and struggling to stay alive.

We'd been talking about the younger days of President Franklin D. Roosevelt, who often sailed over from Campobello to dig at Dark Harbour, Grand Manan, the world's dulse capital, where it was rumoured Captain Kidd's treasure was buried.

We came to a welcome break in the hostile rocky barricade – an open cove with a beach and four fishing corrals or weirs.

"That's Mill Cove," commented Galen. "A man named Dunbar, a master carpenter, lived there in early New Brunswick days. He built the first gallows in Charlotte County at St. Andrews."

"That's interesting."

"Yes – especially because he took all his gold savings and stowed them away, but wouldn't tell his wife where."

"Oh? What did she do?"

"She searched around until she found the money – then she hid it in a new place while he was away in bars drinking."

"And what did he do?"

"Oh, he came home and got mad and killed her," replied Galen matter-of-factly, because it was a long time ago. "Then he cut her up and put her in a pickle barrel in the root cellar under the house."

"How did anyone ever find out?"

"Because he went back to the bars and started boasting about it. The police came and discovered the pickle barrel and arrested him." After a moment's reflective pause Galen added, "He was found guilty and hanged – the first man to be hanged in Charlotte County – on his own gallows."

Ever since then, for a century and a half, he said, men have dug around the Dunbar home without unearthing the missing gold hoard.

"And they say in the dead of night you can hear ghostly screams coming from the old cellar – the screams of Mrs. Dunbar being cut up and put in the pickle barrel."

A moment later he asked, as Mill Cove receded behind us, "Well, what do you think of that?"

To tell the truth, I was thinking I wasn't so sure I still wanted the twelve jars of pickled herring.

But the point of this story is that when I met Galen Sheehan again only three weeks later, he said, "Remember that buried gold of old man Dunbar? They're saying around Campobello that a fellow found Dunbar's rifle the other day while he was just shovelling in the earth – after all that time, too; must be more than a century and a half. They'll all be eager now to find the gold, too." Now, undoubtedly, there will be a renewed swarm of hopeful gold-diggers including the magnetic metal-detector operators who have tried intermittently before.

So it seems that President Roosevelt, as a youthful summer resident sailing over to Grand Manan to look for buried treasure, was digging in the wrong place. He needn't have left Campobello.